Best Of Friends Two

A Cookbook

Written By
Dee Reiser
and
Teresa Dormer

*"More of our best and
gourmet, too"*

Library of Congress #85-90457
ISBN: 0-9615950-4-3

Artwork by *Marshall P. Heintz*
Cover Design by *M.J. Davis*

1st Printing-September, 1987

Quotes scattered throughout this book are sayings picked up over the years and those given to us by special friends. The original sources are unknown. We thank those people, whom-ever they may be.

Printed by
WIMMER BROTHERS
Memphis   Dallas

PREFACE

Our first cookbook "Best of Friends" began through our friendship and love of cooking. It has been a great success because of all of you who bought it for yourselves, told others about it or gave it as a gift to friends or relatives. Many of those who have puchased and used our book have called or written to give lovely comments and compliments and to encourage us toward a second book. We are proud to announce "Here it is."

"Best of Friends Two" is a continuation of our first cookbook with some of our favorite "gourmet" recipes as well. Even the most elegant of these has been simplified and the directions made so explicit that a novice could prepare them; they just take a little more time. We hope that you will be creative and give them a try.

It has been our good fortune to meet so many wonderful people through our travels and promotions and we have made many new friends. We are looking forward to getting to know more of you through this second book.

We have really tried to make this cookbook even better than the first and we feel we have. We hope that you will agree and will continue to enjoy "Our Best" and to encourage all your friends to do the same.

Sharing "our best" and "gourmet", too,

Dee and Teresa

ACKNOWLEDGMENTS

We want to offer our thanks to all of you who have so wholeheartedly supported us. What joy we have experienced from your lovely comments and notes; you were the ones who inspired us to write this second book.

A very special thanks to all our friends who still share their favorite recipes with us, as well as those who really helped us promote our first cookbook. To Bev, Betty Jo, "Mom Helen," Linda, Sam and Joni we say thanks for helping with the proofing of recipes and to Susan, thanks for editing our introductory pages. Thanks also to our new friends that have shared recipes with us. We would never have been as successful without each and every one of you.

To our families—we never could have made it this far without you. We know you had some tough times with our frequent absences, but you "hung in there" with us. Thanks "Mr. Mom" and "Fast Eddie" for holding things together at home. Your love and support of us and pride in our success has been a vital part in the creation of this book. Our graduating seniors Sandra, Susan and Doug have been very understanding during the last week of school while we were working night and day to meet our deadline. Thanks to Jonathan and his buddies for helping with the "testing" of recipes. You're all terrific and we love you!

Thanks to "Papa Joe" for keeping his ideas rolling and cooking in the kitchen with us. He helped us cook up some wonderful dishes for you.

Many, many thanks,

Dee and Teresa

ABOUT THE AUTHORS

We both live in Kingwood, Texas and met through our mutual love of tennis. Before writing our first book, "Best of Friends", we were very active in church activities, needlework, tennis, cooking and entertaining , taking care of our husbands and trying to keep up with our six children.

Since "Best of Friends" was published our tennis and needlework have taken a back seat. Now we stay busy promoting the cookbook. This includes a lot of traveling as well as a first trip to the wholesale market. We've learned how to survive on a few hours sleep and to juggle schedules to make every minute count.

Our families are glad we started test-cooking again; they missed home-cooked meals while we were traveling so much. They really enjoy our "recipe testing" as do our good friends who allowed themselves to be our guinea pigs. Sometimes we had a little more honesty than we wanted, right guys? However, thanks to all, we've come up with a real winner. "Best of Friends Two" will certainly teach us how to handle an even tighter schedule.

Dee and Teresa

Contents

*Many of our recipes use Panola Sauce.
If this is unavailable in your area, your
favorite hot sauce may be substituted.

Appetizers
And
Beverages

SWISS PETITES

2½ cups shredded Swiss
  cheese
⅓-½ cup chopped green
  onion
½ lb. bacon (cooked and
  crumbled)
Dash salt and white
  pepper
Garlic powder to taste
Petite (Cocktail) Rye
Paprika
Hellman's mayonnaise

Mix and make very moist with Hellman's. Spread on Petite Rye. Sprinkle with paprika. Put under broiler until bubbly. This can be fixed ahead and refrigerated until ready to serve. Do not cook before refrigerating. Makes 24.

This comes from a very nice lady, Nancy, that I met while doing a "Tasting" at one of the shops carrying our first cookbook. Our friendships have grown through the first book and we hope they will continue to grow through this one. Thanks, Nancy—everyone loves this! I will double the recipe from now on; people really go nuts over it.

ARTICHOKE DIP

12 oz cream cheese
1 cup mayonnaise
1½-2 packages Good
  Season's Italian dressing
1 can artichoke hearts

Place all ingredients in food processor or blender and process until smooth. Refrigerate at least 2 hours before serving.

MOREDADDY'S PIMIENTO CHEESE SPREAD

1¼ lbs. sharp Cheddar
  cheese, grated
2 (4 oz) jars pimientos,
  drained
1 (8 oz) jar Pace Picante
  Sauce
Fresh ground pepper
3 Tbsp. mayonnaise

Combine thoroughly. Store in refrigerator. Good on crackers or bread.

This comes from my mom. Thanks, Helen.

A true friend is forever a friend.

CHEESE IN A BREAD BOWL

1½ lb. grated sharp
  Cheddar cheese
¼ lb. blue cheese
1 tsp. dry mustard
2 Tbsp. soft margarine
1 tsp. Worcestershire sauce
2 tsp. grated onion
½ tsp. garlic salt
12 oz beer
3 lb. loaf round rye bread
Paprika
Parsley

Hollow out bread, reserve and slice thin. Saw-tooth around the crust edges. Combine cheeses, dry mustard, margarine, Worcester-shire, onion, and garlic salt in a large bowl. Let set for 30 minutes to soften. Add beer slowly and beat until fluffy. Fill bread with this mixture. Garnish with paprika and parsley. Refrigerate. Serve on a large wooden board with reserved rye and crackers.

HOT ARTICHOKE DIP

1 can artichoke hearts,
  drained and chopped
1 cup Hellman's
  mayonnaise
1 cup Parmesan cheese
1 small can green chilies,
  drained

Mix all ingredients together; place in a greased baking dish and bake in a 350° oven for 45 minutes. Serve with crackers.

Another great recipe from Aunt Loreta!

STUFFED ARTICHOKE HEARTS

5 cans artichoke hearts
8 oz cream cheese,
  softened
⅓ cup finely chopped
  green onions
½ tsp. garlic salt
¼ tsp. coarsely ground
  black pepper
⅛ tsp. cayenne
McCormick lemon-pepper
1 stick margarine, melted
Freshly grated Parmesan
  cheese

Drain artichoke hearts and slice off bottom so that hearts can stand upright. Combine cream cheese, green onion, garlic salt, black pepper and cayenne. Open center of artichoke a little bit, sprinkle with lemon-pepper, and put an even amount of cream cheese mixture in each heart. Roll hearts in melted butter and then Parmesan cheese. Place in a greased oven-proof dish and bake at 400° for 15 minutes or until hot and bubbly.

Don't hesitate to assemble in advance. Simply cover and refrigerate until ready to bake. Makes 40.

This can also be used as a vegetable dish.

BOURSIN SPREAD

2 (8 oz) cream cheese
1 (8 oz) whipped, unsalted
  butter
1 tsp. garlic powder
½ tsp. seasoned pepper
1½ tsp. oregano
¼ tsp. dill weed
¼ tsp. thyme
¼ tsp. marjoram
¼ tsp. basil
¼ tsp. seasoned salt

Blend together and mold. Chill.

Jonathan says this is a real winner. Thanks for the tip, Betty Jo!

B. J.'S VEGGIE DIP

1 pint mayonnaise
1 pint sour cream
3 Tbsp. parsley, chopped
3 Tbsp. minced green
  onions
3 Tbsp. dill weed
1½ Tbsp. seasoned salt

Mix all ingredients together and chill. Serve with fresh vegetables.

ZIPPY CHOPPED BEEF SPREAD

8 oz cream cheese
2 tsp. purple onion
1 Tbsp. Pickapeppa sauce
1 Tbsp. horseradish
1 Tbsp. sour cream
½ tsp. seasoned salt
½ tsp. garlic powder
2 oz pkg. chopped beef

Mix all ingredients (except beef) thoroughly until well blended. Shape into a ball and chill. Shred beef and place on wax paper, remove ball from refrigerator and cover with the beef. Chill. Serve with rye or wheat crackers.

This was a hit the first try!

The true friend seeks to give, not to take.

BLACK BEAN DIP

3 cans Progresso Black
  Beans
6 slices bacon, fried crisp
1½ medium onions, finely
  chopped
1 large bell pepper, finely
  chopped
1 tsp. garlic powder
1 tsp. ground cumin
Salt and pepper to taste
2 Tbsp. picante sauce
½ tsp. sugar
Sour cream
Green onions, finely
  chopped
Grated Cheddar cheese

Put beans in food processor; process until finely chopped. Saute onion and bell pepper in bacon drippings. Add beans to onion mixture; add seasonings. Simmer until flavors blend and mixture thickens, stirring often. (20-30 minutes) Place in greased dish; heat in oven at 350° for 20-30 minutes or until hot. Top with sour cream, onion and cheese. Serve with chips. Can be frozen but do not bake before freezing.

This is very good and so easy.

DIETER'S DIP

16 oz plain yogurt
1 package Ranch
  buttermilk dressing mix
1 cup Hellman's light
  mayonnaise

Beat together with a whisk. Serve as a dip with fresh vegetables or as a salad dressing. Great on baked potatoes as well.

AUNT LORETA'S HERB DIP

1 cup mayonnaise
½ Tbsp. lemon juice
¼ tsp. salt
¼ tsp. paprika
1 tsp. minced dried herbs
1 tsp. dried onion flakes
1 tsp. minced dried parsley
½ tsp. garlic powder
⅛-¼ tsp. curry powder
1 cup sour cream

Mix ingredients in order given, stirring thoroughly. Serve with vegetables-carrots, bell pepper, cauliflower, radishes and broccoli are all good.

This dip is also good as a dressing on salad and on hamburgers. Tip: Make at least 3-4 hours before serving so flavors have time to blend.

BLACK-EYED PEA DIP

1¾ cups dried black-eye
  peas
5 cups water
5 jalapeno peppers,
  seeded & chopped
⅓ cup chopped onion
1 clove garlic
1 cup butter
2 cups shredded sharp
  American cheese
4 oz can chopped green
  chiles
1 Tbsp. jalapeno pepper
  liquid

Sort and wash peas; place in a heavy saucepan, cover with water and bring to a boil. Cook 2 minutes, remove from heat. Cover and soak 1 hour; drain. Combine peas and 5 cups water, bring to a boil. Reduce heat, cover, simmer 1¼ hours or until tender. Drain. Combine peas, jalapenos, onion and garlic in blender. Blend until smooth-set aside. Combine butter and cheese in top of a double boiler-bring water to a boil. Reduce heat to low-cook, stirring occasionally until melted. Add chiles, pepper liquid and pea mixture. Stir well. Serve with corn chips.

CHERYL'S TAMALE DIP
Microwave

2 cans Hormel Chili (no
  beans) ⋆
2 cans Hormel Tamales
1 small jar Cheez Whiz

Mash tamales. Add chili; mix well. Heat in microwave for 2-3 minutes-stir. Add Cheez Whiz; heat until hot. Serve with tortillo snacks or chips.

This comes from our very special friend, Mary. Her boys call this Frito Pie. It's really good and so easy!!

⋆ To add spice, use 1 can hot chili.

TERRIYAKI MEATBALLS

3 lbs. ground chuck
5 oz soy sauce
2 oz oil
3 cloves crushed garlic
1 tsp. ginger
1 tsp. dry mustard
1 Tbsp. brown sugar

Make small meatballs with the ground chuck. Place in a flat roasting pan. Mix remaining ingredients and pour over the meatballs. Cook uncovered for 1 hour at 275°.

CHILI-CHEESE DIP

4 Tbsp. margarine
⅓ cup chopped green
  onion
¼ tsp. garlic powder
¼ tsp. cayenne
½ tsp. black pepper
4½ tsp. red Panola Sauce
1 tsp. Konriko
1 can (1 lb. 3 oz) Ranch
  Style Chili (no beans)
1 can Cream of Mushroom
  soup
1 lb. Mexican Velveeta
  (hot)
1 8 oz package Monterey
  Jack cheese

Melt margarine in a 3 qt. saucepan. Saute green onion and garlic powder in margarine until soft. Add seasonings, chili, and soup, stirring well. Add cheeses which have been cut into cubes. Stir over low heat until all cheese is melted. Adjust seasonings. Serve with chips.

My teenagers love this. If you don't like things spicy, omit the Panola Sauce and cayenne.

CHILI-TAMALE DIP

3 Tbsp. margarine
1 large onion, finely
  chopped
½ tsp. garlic powder
1½ tsp. chili powder
½ tsp. Worcestershire
1 can tamales, mashed
1 can chili, without beans
2-3 cups shredded sharp
  Cheddar cheese

Saute onion and garlic in margarine; add remaining ingredients. Stir until cheese is melted; adjust seasoning. Serve with chips. This is addictive! Also good on hot dogs.

A friend is one who knows who you are, understands where you've been, accepts who you've become, and still gently invites you to grow.

FESTIVE CHEESE DIP

3 Tbsp. margarine
½ cup chopped green
   onion
¼ tsp. garlic powder
¼ tsp. Konriko
½ tsp. red Panola Sauce
1-1½ tsp. Picante Sauce ★
1 can (10 oz) Rotel diced
   Tomatoes & Green
   Chilies
1 lb. Mexican Velveeta, cut
   in chunks ★
4 oz Monterey Jack
cheese, cut in chunks
½ cup sour cream

Saute green onions in margarine. Add remaining ingredients in order given, *stirring constantly* until cheese is melted and smooth. Use medium to low heat. Great with tortillo chips.

★ My gang likes the hot Picante and Velveeta, but for those who don't like hot spices, use the mild.

This dip has been a winner with everyone I've tried it on.

GUACAMOLE DIP

3 ripe avocados
1 (8 oz) pkg. cream cheese
1 tsp. salt
Juice of ½ lemon
1 tomato, peeled and
   chopped
½-1 tsp. garlic salt
¼ tsp. pepper
Dash Worcestershire sauce
⅓-½ cup hot Picante
   sauce

Put all ingredients in food processor or blender until smooth.

This is one of "T's" creations and one of my favorites!!

SAUSAGE BISCUITS

3 cups Bisquick
1 lb. hot pork sausage roll
1 lb. grated sharp Cheddar
   cheese
2 Tbsp. Panola Sauce or to
   taste
½ tsp. garlic powder

Mix all ingredients together and form into golf ball-size balls. Bake on a cookie sheet at 375° for 15-20 minutes or until nicely browned.

Thanks to Panola Sauce, this is a great variation of an old favorite!

SWEDISH MEATBALLS

Meatballs:
1 lb. ground chuck
½ lb. ground pork
2 eggs
1 tsp. salt
Pinch nutmeg
1 Tbsp. finely chopped
   onion
1 tsp. minced parsley
½ cup bread crumbs
½ cup milk

Sauce:
3 Tbsp. butter
1 Tbsp. oil
2-4 cloves garlic, minced
1 onion, finely chopped
1 Tbsp. chopped bell
   pepper
1 Tbsp. paprika
Small jar sliced
   mushrooms
2 Tbsp. flour
1 cup beef broth
1 Tbsp. ketchup
½ cup sour cream
1 tsp. Worcestershire sauce
Salt & pepper to taste

Meatballs:
Soak bread crumbs in milk 5 minutes. Combine with remaining ingredients and chill 1 hour. Shape into small balls.

Sauce:
Saute meatballs in butter and oil. Remove. In same pan saute garlic, onion, pepper and mushrooms for 1 minute. Add paprika. Cook until vegetables are tender. Stir in flour, then broth, add ketchup, Worcestershire, salt and pepper. Simmer 5 minutes. Blend some of sour cream into sauce, then add remaining sour cream. Add meatballs, simmer 20 minutes.

SMOKED OYSTER ROLL

8 oz cream cheese
3-5 dashes Worcestershire
2-3 dashes Tabasco
¼ tsp. garlic powder
1 can smoked oysters
Paprika
Parsley

Mix cream cheese, Worcestershire, Tabasco and garlic together thoroughly and spread into a rectangle on waxed paper. Cover with oysters and roll up jellyroll-fashion. Sprinkle top with paprika and garnish with fresh parsley. Serve with crackers.

OYSTERS JOSEPH

1 qt. oysters
Garlic salt
Seasoned pepper
1 package frozen, chopped
  spinach
1 small onion, chopped
4 cloves garlic, minced
1 stalk celery, minced
6 oz can white crabmeat
¼ tsp. oregano
¼ tsp. parsley flakes
Creole seasoning
1 stick margarine
1 cup white sauce
Parmesan cheese

Put 7-8 oysters in a ramekin; sprinkle with garlic salt and seasoned pepper. Broil until oysters begin to curl around the edges. Cook spinach until thawed; mix together with the onion, garlic, celery, crabmeat, oregano and parsley flakes. Put on top of oysters; sprinkle with Creole seasoning and top with a pat of butter. Place in center of oven and broil until butter melts. Remove from oven and place 2-3 Tbsp. cream sauce on top and sprinkle with Parmesan cheese. Broil in lower oven until cheese browns. You may also add boiled shrimp around the edges of the ramekins.

Dad had all of us involved in the making of this dish one Saturday afternoon while he was here visiting. Even Sam and Ed were helping!

JOE'S RED-HOT SALSA

⅛ tsp. sugar
6 large tomatoes, peeled
½ tsp. crushed red pepper
6 fresh jalapenos, cut in
  slices
2 large cloves garlic, cut in
  four pieces
1 medium onion, cut in 6
  pieces
1 Tbsp. olive oil
1½ tsp. cilantro, freshly
  chopped
Salt and pepper to taste

Puree tomatoes with sugar and red pepper in processor. Pour into bowl. In processor, coarsely chop jalapenos, garlic and onion; add to tomatoes along with olive oil and salt and pepper to taste. Add cilantro and stir well.

This is very hot but very good. Great just with chips or with eggs or as a condiment to any food.

A friend is someone who makes time to get together when there is no time.

JERRY'S SALSA

1 can (1 lb. 12 oz) tomatoes, drained and finely chopped
1 cup onion, finely chopped
2 cans (4 oz) green chilies, drained and finely chopped
1 tsp. chopped natural garlic ★
2 Tbsp. safflower oil
¼ tsp. salt
¼ tsp. pepper
¼ tsp. chili powder
12 oz tomato sauce
1 Tbsp. jalapeno pepper, finely chopped

In medium saucepan, combine all ingredients and mix well. Bring to boiling, stirring. Reduce heat and simmer 20 minutes, stirring occasionally. Refrigerate, covered, for 1-2 days. To serve, allow salsa to come to room temperature or serve cold.
Make 2½ cups.

★ Natural garlic comes in a small jar and is usually found in the fresh produce section of your grocery store. Jerry recommends using it in this recipe.

Jerry is a neighbor and good friend. He loves to cook and is always working on something new. Thanks for sharing, Jerry.

PAM'S TRASH

1 box Cheese Nips
1 box Cheese Tidbits
1 box Pretzels
1 box Corn Bran
1 box Rice Chex
1 box Corn Chex or Crispix
1 box Cheerios
Nuts (optional) ★
3 cups oil
4 Tbsp. Worcestershire sauce
2 Tbsp. garlic salt
2 Tbsp. seasoned salt
1-2 Tbsp. Tabasco
1-2 Tbsp. Pickapeppa Sauce
1-2 Tbsp. cayenne

Mix in very large roaster. Bake at 250° for 2 hours, stirring every 15 minutes.
Makes 9 quarts.

★ Pam doesn't put the nuts in her Trash. She says, "When I eat nuts, I eat nuts. When I eat Trash, I eat Trash!" Thanks for the recipe, Pam, we love you.

 Life is nothing without friendship.

MARINATED VEGETABLES

4 oz red wine vinegar
¼ cup vegetable oil
¼ cup olive oil
2 Tbsp. sugar
1 Tbsp. salt
½ tsp. oregano
½ tsp. basil
½ tsp. garlic powder
¼ cup water
¼ tsp. pepper
2 carrots, peeled & sliced
2 celery stalks, sliced
1 small cauliflower,
   separated into flowerets
1 bell pepper, cut into
   chunks
2 cups broccoli flowerets
1 jar whole mushrooms
1 can ripe olives

In a large skillet, combine first 10 ingredients; add carrots. Cover and simmer 2 minutes. Add celery, cauliflower and broccoli; cover and simmer 2 more minutes. Add remaining ingredients; cover and simmer 1 more minute. Refrigerate for 24 hours. Drain and serve with toothpicks. The vegetables will be crisp. If you like them softer, simmer a little longer.

HOT CRAB SPREAD

8 oz cream cheese
1 Tbsp. half & half
6½ oz can crabmeat
2 tsp. minced onion
½ tsp. horseradish
¼ tsp. salt
¼ tsp. pepper
1 tsp. Worcestershire sauce
1 tsp. Creole seasoning

Mix together and bake at 325° for 10-15 minutes. Serve with crackers.

PANOLA CHEESE SPREAD

8 oz pkg. cream cheese
2-3 oz Panola Sauce
1 small jar orange or
   pineapple marmalade

Place cheese on tray, top with marmalade of your choice. Then top with Panola Sauce. Serve with your favorite crackers.

SHRIMP MOLD

1 can tomato soup
8 oz cream cheese, softened
2 envelopes unflavored gelatin
¼ cup lukewarm water
2 lbs. shrimp, boiled, peeled and finely chopped
1 cup minced celery
½ cup minced onion
½ cup minced green onion
6-8 drops Tabasco
¾ cup mayonnaise
¼ cup seafood cocktail sauce

Heat soup and add cream cheese. Stir with a whisk until smooth. Dissolve gelatin in water and add to soup. Stir in remaining ingredients. Pour into a well-greased 4-cup mold. Refrigerate until set. Unmold and invert on a serving dish. Serve with Triscuit and Escort crackers.
Serves 16.

This is so much better if you really spice up your water when boiling the shrimp. I always add lemon juice, garlic, salt, pepper, Worcestershire, Tabasco and Creole seasoning.

SHRIMP PUFFS

Puff:
1 stick butter
1 cup water
1 cup flour
½ tsp. salt
4 eggs

Filling:
½ cup finely minced celery
1½ cups chopped, boiled shrimp
2 cups grated sharp Cheddar cheese
1½-2 cups mayonnaise
2 Tbsp. Worcestershire sauce
1 Tbsp. Tabasco
4 green onions, minced
½ tsp. garlic powder
¼ tsp. Creole seasoning
Salt and pepper to taste

Puff:
Place water and butter in a saucepan; bring to a boil over medium heat. Add flour and salt; reduce to low and stir until mixture leaves the side of the pan. Remove from heat. Stir in eggs, one at a time, beating well after each. Drop ½ teaspoonfuls onto a lightly greased baking sheet. Bake at 400° for 20-30 minutes or until light golden brown. (These may be frozen and filled later.)

Filling:
Combine all ingredients and chill. Cut off the top of each puff, fill with mixture and replace top. Place on a baking sheet and warm until the cheese melts in a 350° oven.
Makes 45-50.

If you'd prefer you could replace the shrimp with crabmeat or chicken.

OYSTERS BROCHETTE

10 slices bacon (thick
  sliced)
36 raw oysters
Flour, seasoned with salt,
  pepper, cayenne and
  Konriko creole
  seasoning
⅓ cup butter
⅓ cup oil
⅓ cup bacon grease
Crushed red pepper to
  taste
12 toast triangles
1 tsp. chopped parsley
2 tsp. chopped green
  onions
1 tsp. lemon or lime juice
Garlic powder

Cut bacon into 1" pieces and fry until partially cooked on both sides; drain and reserve drippings. On skewers, string 6 pieces of bacon alternately with 6 oysters. Roll in seasoned flour and sprinkle with garlic powder. Heat butter, oil and bacon grease in a skillet with crushed red pepper; saute oysters and bacon on all sides until done. Lay each skewer on 2 toast triangles. Add parsley, green onions and lemon juice to remaining oil in skillet; blend and heat well. Pour a little over each portion.
Serves 6.

INSTANT SPICED TEA MIX

2 cups Tang
½ cup sugar
1 large pre-sweetened Kool
  Aid lemonade mix
½ cup instant tea
½ tsp. cinnamon
1 tsp. cloves

Combine all ingredients well and store in a covered jar. Place 2-3 teaspoons in a mug, fill with boiling water. You can make this low calorie by using sugar-free Tang and lemonade mix and substituting Equal for the sugar.

We drink this all winter long, you don't have to worry about your vitamin C.

A friend is one with whom you share
your choicest thoughts.

HOT SPICED TEA

1 gallon water
3 cinnamon sticks
5 cloves
3 family-size tea bags
6 oz can orange juice
6 oz can lemonade
½-1 cup sugar

Boil water with cinnamon sticks and cloves; add tea bags and steep for 10 minutes. Remove spices. Add orange juice, lemonade and sugar. Good hot or cold.

ORANGE FROTH

6 oz can frozen orange juice
1 can water
1 can milk
½ cup sugar
1 tsp. vanilla
11 ice cubes

Place all ingredients in blender and blend until smooth and frothy. Serve immediately.

ORANGE CHAMPAGNE COCKTAIL

1 bottle chilled champagne
1 bottle chilled ginger ale
2 cups orange juice
Strawberries

Combine champagne, ginger ale and juice and mix well. Pour into glasses and top with sliced strawberries.

FREEZER DAQUIRIS

1½ cups rum
1½ cups vodka
12 oz can frozen limeade
12 oz can frozen lemonade
2 (28 oz) Sprite

Mix all together and freeze at least 2 days

A refreshing treat to help offset these hot, humid Houston days!

HOT BUTTERED RUM

1 lb. butter
16 oz light brown sugar
16 oz powdered sugar,
  sifted
2 tsp. ground cinnamon
2 tsp. ground nutmeg
1 qt. softened vanilla ice
  cream
Light rum
Whipped cream
Cinnamon sticks

Combine butter, sugar and spices, beat until light and fluffy. Add ice cream and stir until well blended. Spoon mixture into a freezer container and freeze.

To serve: Thaw slightly, place 3 tablespoons butter mixture and 1 jigger of rum into a large mug. Fill with boiling water and stir well. Top with whipped cream and add a cinnamon stick.
Makes 25 cups.

(Mixture may be refrozen).

DORENE'S PEACH KISS

½ Peach Schnapps
½ seltzer water
2-3 frozen peach slices

Pour Schnapps and seltzer over frozen peach slices in a glass and serve.

A nice summer drink.

WINDJAMMERS

3 (46 oz) cans pineapple
  juice
2 (12 oz) cans orange juice
2 orange juice cans water
2¾ cups rum
2 cups Amaretto
1 jar cherries

Mix all together, pour over a block of ice.

Thanks Joni, this is a good one!

BERRY'S SANGRIA

3½ cups wine (red or
    white)
½ cup sugar
½ cup vodka
1 lime
10 oz club soda

In 2 quart pitcher, put wine, sugar and vodka. Stir well, add juice of lime plus lime itself and then club soda. Add enough ice cubes to fill to 2 quart level. Stir and serve. Tastes so good you may forget it has a "kick". The white wine is especially good in the summer months; it's very refreshing. The red wine is heavier and we serve it more in the winter. Both can be served at anytime, though.

This comes from our very dear friends, Bill and Roberta. Thanks so much for sharing it with us. Watch it, Berta, Sam can still pour through fingers!

LINDA'S SPECIAL COFFEE

1 oz Brandy
1 Tbsp. Kahlua
Hot coffee
Whipped cream
Brown sugar
Lime juice

Frost cup with lime juice and brown sugar. In cup, pour Brandy and Kahlua; fill remainder of cup with hot coffee. Top with whipped cream and a sprinkling of brown sugar.
Serves 1.

Thanks Linda, what a treat!

 A friend is worth all the hazards we can run.

Bread

TERRIFIC DINNER ROLLS

l pkg. dry yeast
l cup warm water
5 Tbsp. sugar
l tsp. salt
3 cups flour
4 Tbsp. butter or
    margarine, melted and
    cooled
l egg, beaten
Melted butter or margarine

Dissolve yeast in warm water. In a large mixing bowl, combine yeast mixture, sugar, salt and l cup flour. Beat with mixer; add butter and egg, beat again. Add second cup of flour; beat well. Add last cup ⅓ at a time, beating after each ⅓. Using the mixer really takes all the work out of it. Let rise in same bowl until doubled. Turn onto floured board and work in enough flour to make dough easy to handle. Roll to ½" thickness and cut with small biscuit cutter. Dip rolls in melted butter and place in pan. (I use 2-9" cake pans). Let rise again until doubled. Bake in preheated 375° oven for 10-12 minutes or until done. These freeze well but you probably won't have any left to freeze. They are great!
Makes 2-3 dozen, depending on size biscuit cutter.

BUTTERED HORNS

1¼ cups milk
l tsp. salt
½ cup sugar
l pkg. dry yeast dissolved
    in a little warm water
½ cup shortening, melted
    and cooled
4 cups flour (may take a
    little more)
2 eggs
1½-2 sticks butter, melted
    and cooled

Scald milk; pour over sugar and salt mixture. Add yeast-then half of flour. Add shortening, unbeaten eggs and remaining flour. Place in greased bowl and let rise until double in bulk. Divide into 3 pieces-roll into circles and spread with melted butter. Cut in pie-shaped wedges and roll up. Place on greased pans-brush with melted butter-cover with waxed paper and damp towel. Let rise until double. Bake at 375° for 15-20 minutes. Delicious!
Makes 3 dozen.

This recipe comes from a very dear friend, Barbara. She's a great lady and wonderful cook. Try these and you'll agree.

SOUR CREAM YEAST ROLLS

2 pkgs. dry yeast
½ cup warm water
(105°-115°)
1 (8 oz) carton sour cream
1 cup butter or margarine,
softened
2 eggs, beaten
⅓ cup sugar
1 tsp. salt
4 cups flour

Dissolve yeast in water; let stand 5 minutes. Place sour cream in a small saucepan; heat on low to 105°. Combine sour cream, butter, eggs, sugar and salt in a large bowl; add yeast mixture and stir well. Gradually stir in flour. Place dough in a well-greased bowl, turning to grease top. Cover and let rise in refrigerator at least 6 hours. (Dough may stay in frig for 24 hours. It rises slightly but does not double in bulk.) Divide dough into 4 equal parts. Roll each part into a 12" circle on floured surface; cut each circle into 12 pie-shaped wedges. Roll up each wedge tightly, beginning at wide end. Seal points, and place rolls, point side down, on greased baking sheets. Curve rolls into a crescent shape. Cover rolls, let rise in a warm place about 30-40 minutes. Bake in upper ⅓ of oven at 375° for 12 minutes.
Makes 4 dozen.

These rolls have a wonderful texture. We had them at one of our Gourmet dinners and we were fighting over them. There's a story behind that but I won't embarrass Bev by telling it. The rolls are terrific!

REFRIGERATOR BISCUITS

3 cups self-rising flour
1½ tsp. baking powder
1 Tbsp. sugar
1 cup shortening
Milk
Melted butter

Sift dry ingredients together and cut in shortening until evenly distributed. At this point you can store in the refrigerator up to 2 weeks. For 6 large biscuits, combine 1 cup mix with enough milk to moisten. Knead on a floured surface 5 to 6 times. Roll out to ½ inch and cut. Place on a cookie sheet and brush tops with melted butter. Place close together for soft biscuits or 1 inch apart for crusty ones. Bake at 450° for 8-10 minutes.

These are very good and make up quickly.

SOFT BREADSTICKS

2½ cups flour
1 package yeast
1 Tbsp. sugar
1½ tsp. salt
1¼ cups warm water
1 Tbsp. oil
1 cup grated Parmesan
   cheese
1 tsp. garlic powder
¾ stick melted margarine
¾ cup Parmesan cheese
Garlic salt with parsley

Combine 1½ cups flour, yeast, sugar and salt in a large mixing bowl; add water and oil. Beat at medium speed 3-4 minutes. Stir in one cup Parmesan cheese, garlic powder and remaining flour. Turn out on a lightly floured surface and knead 4-5 times. Divide dough into fourths and shape each into a ball. Cut each ball into 8 pieces and shape each into an 8-inch long rope. Dip each into melted margarine and then Parmesan cheese. Sprinkle lightly with garlic salt if desired. Place on greased baking sheets 2 inches apart. Cover and let rise for 50 minutes in a warm place (dough will not double). Bake at 400° for 8-12 minutes.

ASPHODEL BREAD

5 cups Pioneer Biscuit Mix
4 Tbsps. sugar
½ tsp. salt
2 envelopes yeast
2 cups *warm* milk
4 eggs
¼ tsp. cream of tartar

Sift into a very large bowl the biscuit mix, sugar and salt. Soften the yeast in milk (if the milk is too warm it will kill the yeast). Beat eggs with the cream of tartar until thoroughly broken up. Combine milk and eggs and pour into dry ingredients. *Mix Well* - it will be a heavy sticky mixture. Set aside in a warm place covered with a damp dishtowel. When doubled in bulk, stir down and pile into oiled loaf pans about half-way. Again double the size. Bake at 350° approximately 20 minutes (depending on the size of pan you use, it usually makes 4 to 5 small loaves).

Serve hot with plenty of butter - Delish!!! This freezes well - completely thaw before reheating or the inside may stay cold.

CHEESE BREAD

½ cup milk
½ cup water
½ cup oil
¼ cup sugar
2 tsp. garlic salt or 1 tsp. plain salt
3½ cups flour
2 eggs
1 pkg. dry yeast
1½-2 cups grated Cheddar cheese
1 Tbsp. dill seed

Heat milk, water, oil, sugar and salt over low heat until warm, stirring to blend. Combine 1½ cups flour and the yeast. Add liquid mixture to flour mixture and beat until smooth-2 minutes-medium speed. Blend in eggs. cheese and dill seed. Stir in remaining 2 cups flour to make stiff batter. Beat until smooth and elastic-1 minute. Grease 2-1 lb. coffee cans. Divide batter between, cover and let rise in warm place until ½" below rim. Bake uncovered in preheated 375° oven 30-35 minutes. Tops will be brown. Cool 15 minutes before serving.

CARAWAY CHEESE MUFFINS

2 cups flour
1 Tbsp. baking powder
2 tsp. sugar
1¼ tsp. salt
¼ tsp. dry mustard
1 cup grated sharp Cheddar cheese
1 egg, well beaten
1 cup milk
¼ cup butter, melted and cooled
Caraway seeds

In a bowl, sift together dry ingredients. Stir in cheese. In another bowl, combine egg, milk and butter. Make a well in center of flour mixture-pour in egg mixture all at once. Stir mixture just until combined. Put into well-greased muffin tins, filling ⅔ full-sprinkle tops with caraway seeds and bake in preheated 350° oven for 25-30 minutes or until puffed and golden. Let cool in pan 1 minute before removing.

These are wonderful!

BEER MUFFINS

3 cups Bisquick
1 cup beer
2 Tbsp. sugar

Mix all together and spoon into greased muffin tins. Bake at 400° for 15 minutes.

A very light, airy muffin that is so-o-o easy!

BACON-CHEESE MUFFINS

1½ cups Hungry Jack
  pancake mix
½ cup milk
1 lb. bacon, cooked &
  crumbled
⅓ cup bacon drippings
1 egg
⅓ cup chopped bell
  pepper
⅓ cup chopped green
  onion
8 oz sharp Cheddar cheese

Combine all ingredients, except cheese, mixing well. Grease muffin tins. Spoon mixture into tins. Cut cheese into ½ inch cubes. Press cheese cube into center of each muffin. Bake at 425° for 15-20 minutes.
Makes 12.

CINNAMON ROLLS

7 cups flour
6 Tbsp. sugar
1½ tsp. salt
2 pkgs. dry yeast
1 cup milk
¾ cup water
⅓ cup butter, cut in pieces
3 eggs
½ cup white sugar
½ cup brown sugar
¼ cup cinnamon
½ cup finely chopped nuts
½ cup golden raisins
½ cup butter, melted
2½ cups powdered sugar
5-6 Tbsp. half & half
1 tsp. almond extract

In large bowl, mix 2 cups flour, sugar, salt and yeast. Combine milk, water and butter in a saucepan until 120°. Add liquid slowly to dry ingredients and beat 2 minutes at medium speed with mixer. Add eggs with another ½ cup flour. Add remaining flour slowly, mixer on low, to make a stiff dough. (If you have a dough hook, use it at this point). Beat 2-3 minutes. Place in greased bowl, turning once; cover and let rise until doubled. Combine sugars, cinnamon, nuts and raisins. Punch dough down; divide in half. Roll each half into 14x9" rectangle. Spread with melted butter and cinnamon mixture. Roll jellyroll style; slice in ½" slices and place in greased pans. (I use 2-9x13 pans.) Cover and let rise until doubled in size. Bake in preheated 350° oven for 15-20 minutes. Mix powdered sugar, milk and almond. Glaze rolls while hot.
Makes 3 dozen rolls

I really get the "gold stars" when I make these for Sam!!!

PUMPKIN BREAD

3⅓ cups flour
3 tsp. cinnamon
3 cups sugar
4 eggs
1 cup oil
⅔ cup water
2 tsp. soda
1 tsp. salt
2 cups cooked pumpkin
1 cup white raisins
1 cup chopped pecans
½ cup chopped dates

Combine flour, cinnamon and sugar. Add eggs, oil and water; mix well. Mix soda, salt and pumpkin, add to other mixture. Stir in raisins, nuts, and dates. Pour into 2 greased loaf pans. Bake at 350° for 1 hour and 15 minutes.

This is very good served with soft cream cheese.

CARROT-PINEAPPLE BREAD

1½ cups flour
1 cup sugar
1 tsp. baking powder
1 tsp. soda
1½ tsp. cinnamon
½ tsp. nutmeg
¼ tsp. salt
2 eggs, beaten
1 cup scraped, shredded
   carrots
½ cup oil
8 oz can crushed
   pineapple, undrained
1 tsp. vanilla
½ cup chopped walnuts

Combine first 7 ingredients in a large mixing bowl, stir in remaining ingredients. Beat at medium speed of mixer 2 minutes. Pour into a greased and floured loaf pan. Bake at 350° for 55 minutes or until a toothpick inserted in center comes out clean.

A friend senses when to talk and when
to listen.

LEMON BREAD

½ cup butter
1 cup sugar
2 eggs
1 tsp. lemon peel, dried
2 tsp. water
½ tsp. lemon extract
1½ cups flour
1 tsp. baking powder
Dash salt
½ tsp. nutmeg
½ cup milk
1 cup pecans, finely
  chopped
¾ cup powdered sugar
2 Tbsp. lemon juice
¼ tsp. lemon extract

Cream butter and sugar until light. Beat in eggs. Combine lemon peel, water and ½ tsp. lemon extract; add to creamed mixture. Sift flour, baking powder, salt and nutmeg; add ⅓ at a time, alternately with the milk, to the egg and sugar mixture. Fold in pecans. Pour into buttered 8x4x2 pan and bake at 350° for 45-55 minutes or 3 mini-loaf pans for 35-40 minutes. Mix powdered sugar, lemon juice and ¼ tsp. lemon extract. Remove bread from oven and while still hot, pour sugar mixture over it. Let cool in pan.

APPLE MUFFINS

1 egg
½ cup milk
4 Tbsp. melted butter
1 cup peeled and grated
  Granny Smith apple
1½ cups flour
½ cup sugar
½ tsp. cinnamon
¼ tsp. nutmeg
2 tsp. baking powder
½ tsp. salt
½ tsp. vanilla
⅓ cup brown sugar
⅓ cup finely minced
  pecans
½ tsp. cinnamon
⅛ tsp. nutmeg

In a bowl beat egg with a fork then stir in milk, butter and apples. In a separate bowl, combine flour, sugar, ½ tsp. cinnamon, ¼ tsp. nutmeg, baking powder and salt. Add to apple mixture, stirring just until flour is moistened. Stir in vanilla. Pour into 12 greased muffin tins. In a small bowl, combine brown sugar, pecans and remaining cinnamon and nutmeg. Sprinkle evenly over each muffin. Bake at 350° for 20-25 minutes.

GREAT BLUEBERRY MUFFINS

2 cups Bisquick
½ cup sugar
1 tsp. cinnamon
½ tsp. nutmeg
1 cup sour cream
1 egg, unbeaten
1 cup fresh blueberries

Topping:
¼ cup brown sugar
½ tsp. cinnamon

Combine Bisquick, sugar, cinnamon and nutmeg; mix well. Make a well in the mixture; add sour cream and egg all at once. Beat with a fork until well mixed. Gently fold in blueberries. Pour into greased muffin tins and sprinkle with brown sugar and cinnamon. Bake at 425° for 20 minutes.
Makes 12 muffins.

Be prepared. Everyone will want the recipe. I always make a double batch or I don't get any.

BRAN MUFFINS

15 oz Raisin Bran (or 2 cups All Bran & 2 cups Raisin Bran)
3 cups sugar
5 cups flour
5 tsp. baking soda
2 tsp. salt
2 Tbsp. apple pie spice
4 beaten eggs
1 cup oil
2 Tbsp. vanilla extract
1 quart buttermilk

Mix all dry ingredients. Add all liquids except eggs. Mix well-add eggs. Bake at 400° for 15-20 minutes in greased muffin tins. Batter will keep in refrigerator up to 6 weeks.

Go wild—add dates, nuts, coconut, etc. These are some of the best muffins ever. Thanks Beverly Elise!

MARY'S LOST BREAD

Stale bread
5 eggs
½ cup sugar
½ cup milk (can use canned milk)
1 tsp. vanilla
1 tsp. cinnamon

Adding one egg at a time, beat all ingredients together. Dip bread in mixture; grill in skillet until golden-brown on both sides. Serve with butter and syrup. Another variation is to sprinkle with cinnamon-powdered sugar mixture.

JAM MUFFINS

½ cup butter
1 cup sugar
2 eggs
2 cups flour
2 tsp. cinnamon
1 tsp. nutmeg
1 tsp. baking powder
½ cup lukewarm milk
2 tsp. vinegar
1 cup of your favorite
   preserves

Cream butter and sugar until fluffy. Add eggs and beat well. Sift flour with cinnamon, nutmeg and baking powder. Combine vinegar and milk and add alternately with dry ingredients to butter mixture. Allow to set a few minutes. Stir in preserves and fill greased muffin tins ⅔ full. Bake at 375° for 20 minutes. These reheat well.

GLAZED ALMOND DOUGHNUTS

1 pkg. dry yeast
2 Tbsp. warm water
¾ cup warm milk
¼ cup sugar
½ tsp. salt
1 tsp. almond extract
½ tsp. vanilla extract
1 egg
3 Tbsp. shortening
2½ cups bread flour
Vegetable oil

Glaze:
2 cups sifted powdered
   sugar
¼ cup milk
¼ tsp. almond extract

Optional:
Sprinkle with finely
   chopped toasted
   almonds

Dissolve yeast in warm water in a large mixing bowl. Add milk, sugar, salt, extracts, egg, shortening and 1 cup flour. Beat on medium speed until well blended. On low speed, add remaining flour. Cover and let rise in a warm place until doubled, about 1 hour. Punch dough down and knead 3-4 times on a well floured surface. Roll to ½ inch thickness and cut with a doughnut cutter. Place on a lightly floured pan. Cover and let rise in a warm place about 30 minutes or until doubled. Heat 3" of oil to 350° and fry 4-5 doughnuts at a time. Cook until golden and turn to other side, repeat. Drain well. Dip warm doughnuts in glaze and cool on wire racks.
Makes 1½ dozen.

These are delicious when freshly made. They are not as good as leftovers as they do not heat well.

FROZEN KOLACKY

½ lb. butter
½ lb. cream cheese
2 cups flour
1 cup powdered sugar
2 tsp. baking powder
1 can Solo filling (flavor
   of your choice)

Work butter and cheese. Sift together flour, sugar and baking powder. Blend well with butter and cheese mixture. Form into 2" diameter rolls; wrap in wax paper. Chill until firm. Cut into ¼" slices. Make a center indention with thumb and fill with filling. Bake at 400° for 10 minutes. Sprinkle with additional powdered sugar.

Solo fillings are found with the fruits and pie fillings. There are quite a few different fillings, now. Poppy seed, prune, apricot and cherry are my favorites. I usually use 3 different kinds when I make this pastry. The filling freezes well so I don't have to worry about wasting it. These are delicious, thanks Ginny. They're great for breakfast, brunch, afternoon tea or even a bedtime snack.

CINNAMON SWIRL COFFEE CAKE

2 cups sugar
1 cup butter
4 eggs
1 cup sour cream
1 tsp. almond extract
1 tsp. vanilla extract
2¼ cups flour
1½ tsp. baking powder
½ tsp. baking soda
Dash salt
1 cup chopped pecans
3 Tbsp. brown sugar
1½ Tbsp. white sugar
2½ tsp. cinnamon
1 tsp. nutmeg

Cream butter and sugar; add eggs, sour cream, almond and vanilla. Set aside. Sift flour, baking powder, soda and salt; add to creamed mixture. Combine pecans, sugars, cinnamon and nutmeg. Pour ⅓ creamed mixture in greased 10" tube pan, ⅓ sugar mixture; repeat twice. With knife, swirl through batter to give marbled effect. Bake at 350° for 40-45 minutes.
Serves 12.

My family loves this. It's really good warm or cold. Sam says I can fix it anytime.

CRUMB CAKE

1½ cups flour
½ cup sugar
2 tsp. baking powder
½ tsp. salt
1 egg
⅔ cup milk
3 Tbsp. oil

Crumb Topping:
¼ stick plus 1 tsp.
   margarine (at room
   temperature)
½ cup sugar
½ cup flour
1 cup *fresh* bread crumbs★
1 tsp. cinnamon
Powdered sugar

Mix flour, sugar, baking powder and salt together. Beat egg with fork, add milk and oil. Stir liquids into dry ingredients mixing only enough to dampen all the flour. Pour into greased 12" pizza pan. Add Crumb Topping and bake 15 minutes at 425°.

Crumb Topping:
Cream margarine; add sugar, flour, crumbs and cinnamon and mix well. (Better if mixed with hands.) In lumps, crumble over batter. Gently press crumbs into batter with palm of your hand. When cake is cooled, sprinkle with powdered sugar.

★ The food processor is great for this.

This recipe comes from a very sweet young lady, Jan, who is very special to our family. It is an old family recipe. Thank you, Jan, for sharing it with us. You may want to bake two—One never does it at my house. It's excellent cold or warmed in the microwave. Bake one at a time-baking two together, one browns too quickly.

APPLE CREAM COFFEE CAKE

½ cup butter
1 cup sugar
2 eggs
1 tsp. vanilla
2 cups flour
1 tsp. baking powder
1 tsp. soda
½ tsp. salt
1 cup sour cream
1 apple, sliced thin
½ cup chopped pecans
2 tsp. cinnamon
1 Tbsp. sugar

Grease tube pan. Cream butter and sugar; add eggs, one at a time. Beat well after each addition. Add vanilla and dry ingredients, sour cream and apples. Spread ½ batter in pan. Mix pecans, cinnamon and sugar together. Sprinkle ½ nut mixture on top of batter; repeat layers. Bake at 275° for 40 minutes.

Another of Helen's great recipes—thanks, Mom!

BLUEBERRY BUNDT DELIGHT

1¼ cups fresh blueberries
⅓ cup sugar
2 Tbsp. cornstarch
1 tsp. almond extract
½ cup softened butter
1 cup sugar
2 eggs
2 cups flour
1 tsp. baking powder
1 tsp. soda
½ tsp. salt
8 oz sour cream
1 tsp. almond extract
½ cup finely chopped,
  sliced almonds
Glaze (recipe follows)

Glaze:
¾ cup sifted, powdered
  sugar
1 Tbsp. warm milk
½ tsp. almond extract

Combine blueberries, ⅓ cup sugar, 1 tsp. almond and cornstarch in a small saucepan. Cook on low 2-3 minutes until thickened, stirring constantly. Set aside. Cream butter; gradually add 1 cup sugar, beating until well blended. Add eggs, one at a time, beating after each addition. Combine flour, baking powder, soda and salt. Add to creamed mixture alternately with sour cream, beginning and ending with flour. Stir in 1 tsp. almond. Spoon half the batter into a greased bundt pan, spoon on half the blueberry mixture and swirl with a knife. Repeat with the remaining batter and blueberry sauce, adding almonds to top. Bake at 350° for 50 minutes or until done. Let stand 5 minutes and remove from pan. Drizzle glaze over the top.

Glaze:
Combine all ingredients, whisking well.

CINNAMON-APPLE PANCAKE

4 Tbsp. butter
1½ cups milk
¾ cup flour
3 eggs
⅓ cups sugar
¼ tsp. salt
3 apples, peeled, cored
  and thinly sliced
1½ tsp. lemon juice
3 Tbsp. brown sugar
¾ tsp. cinnamon
3 Tbsp. butter

In a large glass pie plate melt 4 tablespoons butter in a 400° oven for 5 minutes. Combine milk, flour, eggs, sugar and salt in a blender. Mix on medium speed until smooth. Remove pie plate from oven and increase heat to 450°. Pour batter into pie plate and bake for 20 minutes. Reduce heat to 350° and bake an additional 8 minutes. A well will form in the center. Toss apple slices with lemon juice. Set aside. Mix brown sugar and cinnamon. In a skillet melt butter over medium heat; stir in apples and sprinkle with the sugar mixture. Simmer 15-20 minutes and spoon into the well of pancake.

BLUEBERRY BEGINNING

1½ sticks margarine,
  softened
1 cup sugar
2 eggs
1 cup milk
½ cup sour cream
2 tsp. vanilla
3¼ cups flour
1½ tsp. salt
1 tsp. cinnamon
1 Tbsp. baking powder
2 cups fresh blueberries★

Topping:
1½ sticks margarine,
  melted
½ cup brown sugar
1½ Tbsp. cinnamon
½ tsp. nutmeg

Cream butter and sugar, beat in egg. Blend in milk, sour cream and vanilla. Add flour, salt, cinnamon and baking powder and mix thoroughly. Gently fold in blueberries and pour batter into a greased 9x13 pan. Add topping and bake at 375° for 35-40 minutes. Serves 12.

★Can substitute canned, drained blueberries.

Topping:
Pour melted margarine evenly over batter. Combine cinnamon, sugar and nutmeg and sprinkle over the batter.

A great coffee cake and an excellent way to make points with your hubby.

SANTA FE TOAST

9 slices French bread, ¾"
  thick
6 eggs
1½ cups whipping cream
¼ tsp. salt
⅛ tsp. nutmeg
⅛ tsp. cinnamon
¾ cup oil
Powdered sugar
Syrup

Remove crust from bread; cut each piece diagonally into triangles. Beat eggs lightly with fork; add cream, salt, nutmeg, and cinnamon. Soak triangles until egg mixture is absorbed. (Pour mixture over bread arranged on a cookie sheet). Heat oil in skillet to 350° and fry triangles until golden brown. Drain on paper towels. At this point bread can rest for 45 minutes or can be placed immediately on a cookie sheet lined with foil. Bake at 400° for 3-5 minutes-until puffed. Serve 3 triangles per person on a heated plate. Serve with powdered sugar and syrup.
Serves 6.

BLUEBERRY PANCAKE STACK

Pancakes:
2½ cups milk
4 Tbsp. melted butter
2 eggs, separated
2 cups flour
4 tsp. baking powder
4 Tbsp. sugar
1 tsp. salt

Lemon Cream Butter:
½ cup butter
2½ cups powdered sugar
3 Tbsp. lemon juice
Grated rind of 1 lemon

Blueberry Sauce:
32 oz frozen blueberries
1 cup cold water
3 Tbsp. cornstarch
6 Tbsp. sugar
2 Tbsp. lemon juice

Mix milk, butter and egg yolks. Beat egg whites until stiff. Add whites with remaining ingredients and blend well. Cook and stack. Makes 10-12.

Lemon Cream Butter:
Cream butter, add sugar and beat. Stir in lemon juice and grated rind. Beat until the consistency of whipped cream.

Blueberry Sauce:
Defrost berries, drain and reserve juice. Combine water and juices; add cornstarch and sugar. Cook over low heat until clear and thickened. Add berries and cook 5 minutes. Remove from heat and add lemon juice. (If using fresh berries, you will need to add more sugar).

To Assemble:
Spread a tray with a little lemon butter and top with a pancake. Spread more lemon butter on pancake and a little hot blueberry syrup. Repeat until all pancakes are used; pour remaining syrup over all and dollop top with lemon butter. Bake at 350° for 3 minutes. Cut into wedges to serve. (You may do these individually if you prefer.

A breakfast fit for a king, right B. J.

SOUR CREAM PANCAKES

1 cup flour
¼ tsp. salt
1 Tbsp. sugar
1 Tbsp. baking powder
1 egg
1 cup milk
3 Tbsp. sour cream
2 Tbsp. melted butter

Sift flour with dry ingredients. Beat together egg, milk and sour cream. Combine with flour mixture. Add butter and beat with a whisk until smooth. Drop onto a hot griddle. Make 10-12 light, fluffy pancakes.

These have really spoiled Ed and my boys!

Soup 'n Salads

CREAM OF CELERY SOUP

2 Tbsp. butter
1½ cups thinly sliced
  celery
½ cup thinly sliced onion
3 chicken bouillon cubes
1½ cups hot water
2 Tbsp. flour
1½ cups milk
1 tsp. salt
½ tsp. pepper
1 potato, shredded
2 Tbsp. minced fresh
  parsley
Crumbled bacon (optional)

In a large saucepan melt butter, add onions and celery. Saute on medium until tender. In a bowl dissolve bouillon in hot water; add to pan. Combine flour and milk, add to pot. Add salt, pepper, potato and parsley. Cover and simmer for 45-60 minutes on low heat. Garnish with crumbled bacon if desired.
Serves 4.

CREAM OF CAULIFLOWER SOUP

2 heads cauliflower,
  broken in pieces
5 chicken bouillon cubes
1½ tsp. lime juice
1 stick margarine
1 large onion, chopped fine
½ cup flour
3 cups half and half
Salt, pepper, cayenne,
  garlic powder and
  nutmeg to taste
2½ cups grated cheese,
  Cheddar or Monterey
  Jack

Place cauliflower in large pot and add just enough water to cover; add bouillon and lime juice and bring to a boil. Cook until tender (about 15 minutes); save juice in pot. Puree cauliflower in food processor. Melt margarine in skillet and add onion; cook until tender. Add flour and half-and-half, stirring constantly. Add all ingredients to pot; add seasoning to taste. Simmer a few minutes; add cheese and stir until melted.

Very good—very fast—very easy!

One of the most beautiful qualities of true
friendship is to understand and to
be understood.

CREAM OF EGGPLANT SOUP

1 stick butter
3 cups onion, diced
3 cups celery, diced
2 large eggplants,
  unpeeled and diced
3 cups potatoes, diced
1 tsp. curry powder
1 tsp. thyme
1 tsp. basil
1 tsp. black pepper
Salt to taste
8 cups chicken stock
4 cups whipping cream

Melt butter in 6 quart pot. Saute onion, celery, eggplant and potatoes. Add seasoning and cook, stirring often, until potatoes are tender (10-15 minutes). Stir in stock-cook until mixture thickens (30-40 minutes). Remove from heat; add cream. In batches, put in food processor and puree. Serve immediately.
Serves 12.

CHEESE-BROCCOLI SOUP

1½ lbs. fresh broccoli
1 pint half & half
2 cups water
1 lb. Velveeta
½ tsp. garlic powder
Salt & pepper to taste
½ cup cornstarch mixed
  with 1 cup water

Steam broccoli until tender. Place half & half and water in a double boiler, add cheese, garlic, salt and pepper. Heat until cheese is melted. Add chopped, steamed broccoli. Mix cornstarch and water and add to mixture. Heat over simmering water until soup thickens.
Serves 6.

BROCCOLI SOUP

1 bunch fresh broccoli,
  washed and cut up
1 stalk celery, chopped
1 onion, chopped
3 cups chicken broth
Pinch dry mustard
Salt, pepper to taste
1 cup cream
Freshly grated nutmeg

Combine in a large saucepan the broccoli, celery, onion and broth. Cook until the vegetables are tender; then puree in a blender or processor. Return to saucepan and add the remaining ingredients and heat. (Do Not Boil).
Serves 4.

POTATO SOUP

4 cups peeled and diced
   potatoes
l cup minced celery
½ cup minced onion
½ cup minced green onion
2 cups water
2 tsp. salt
l cup milk
l cup whipping cream
3 Tbsp. melted butter
2 Tbsp. minced fresh
   parsley
½ tsp. pepper
¾ tsp. garlic powder
¼ tsp. Creole seasoning
Garnish: chopped green
   onion-crumbled bacon

Combine potatoes, celery, onions, water and salt in a large saucepan. Simmer, covered, about l5 minutes or until potatoes are tender. Mash vegetables just a little; stir in remaining ingredients. Return to heat and simmer on low about l5-20 minutes. (Do not boil). Garnish with chopped green onions and crumbled bacon.

SPLIT PEA SOUP

4 cups chicken stock
2 lbs. split peas
l medium onion, chopped
l carrot, peeled and
   chopped
Salt, white pepper, and
   garlic powder
l large bay leaf
l cup cubed ham ★
¼ cup heavy cream
Wheat bread
Oil
Butter

In a large pot (4 qt.) combine stock, peas, onion, carrot, seasonings to taste, bay leaf, and ham. Bring to boil and cook until peas are soft. Remove from heat and puree in food processor or blender in batches. Put back in pot and add cream. If soup is too thick, add a little more chicken stock. Heat, adjust seasonings and serve topped with croutons. For croutons, cut slices of wheat bread into cubes (½-l slice per serving). Heat 3 Tbsp. oil and l Tbsp. butter in skillet; add 3 slices bread, cubed, and stir and shake until golden brown. If more is needed, do another batch. These croutons are really good but do not keep well so only fix what you need.

★ If you have a left-over hambone, use it.

CREAM OF CARROT SOUP

2 cups peeled and grated
  carrots
¼ cup butter
½ tsp. salt
½ cup water
2 Tbsp. flour
2¼ cups milk
½ tsp. salt
¼ tsp. white pepper
¼ tsp. ginger
½ tsp. sherry
½ cup whipping cream

Combine carrots, 2 tablespoons butter, ½ teaspoon salt and water in a saucepan. Cover and cook on low for 15-20 minutes or until carrots are done. Set aside. Melt remaining butter in a saucepan over low heat, add flour, stirring until smooth. Cook 1 minute, stirring constantly. Gradually stir in milk; cook over medium heat, stirring constantly, until smooth and thick. Stir in salt, pepper, ginger and sherry, heating through. Add whipping cream, blend well. Cook over low heat, stirring until thoroughly heated. Serve immediately.
Serves 4.

BLACK BEAN SOUP

1 lb. black beans, sorted &
  washed
4-6 cups beef broth
4 cloves garlic, minced
¼ cup margarine
1½ Tbsp. lemon juice
¼ cup rum
Salt, pepper to taste
Sour cream
½ cup finely chopped
  avocado
2 Tbsp. chopped jalapeno
  pepper
1 Tbsp. minced *fresh*
  cilantro
Shredded farmer cheese
Shredded Monterey Jack
  cheese

Combine cleaned beans, broth, garlic and margarine in a large heavy pan. Bring to a boil, reduce heat and simmer until tender, about 2-3 hours. Add additional broth if needed. Mash beans a little, then stir in lemon juice and rum. Add salt and pepper to taste, continue cooking over low heat for 15-20 minutes. Serve topped with sour cream, avocado, jalapeno, cilantro and cheese or a combination of whatever your tastes prefer.
Serves 6-8.

Of all the blessings the Lord sends...friendship
must be his favorite.

SAM'S TURTLE SOUP
(Mock Turtle Variation)

2 lb. turtle meat or 1
  chicken
3 quarts chicken stock
½ cup cooking oil
¼ cup flour
2 large onions, chopped
½ cup bell pepper,
  chopped
½ cup celery, chopped
1 (6 oz) can tomato paste
1 Tbsp. Worcestershire
  sauce
Salt, pepper and garlic
  powder to taste
¼ cup lemon, finely
  chopped, with juice
3 hard-boiled eggs,
  shredded
Sherry

For turtle meat, cut in small cubes and boil in water for 1 hour. (For chicken, cut in pieces-boil for 1 hour-debone and cut in cubes.) Make a roux with oil and flour. Cook, stirring constantly, over medium heat until golden-brown. Saute onion, bell pepper and celery in roux until soft; add tomato paste and fry until brown. Add meat, chicken stock, Worcestershire, salt, pepper, garlic and lemon. Cook over low heat for 1½ hours. Add eggs and cook 30 minutes. To serve, add 1 Tbsp. sherry to soup bowl and ladle soup over it.
Serves 10-12.

This is another of Sam's great recipes. Ask "T" about this one. She loves it.

SHRIMP BISQUE

1 lb. shrimp, boiled &
  peeled
2 cups half & half
4 Tbsp. butter
¼ cup chopped onion
3 green onions, finely
  chopped
2 stalks celery, finely
  chopped
1½ Tbsp. flour
1 tsp. Konriko Creole
  Seasoning
¼ tsp. cayenne
½ tsp. paprika
¼ tsp. garlic powder
1 cup milk
1 cup heavy cream
4 Tbsp. sherry or to taste

Puree shrimp in blender or processor with 1 cup half & half. Set aside. Melt butter-saute onions and celery over medium heat until cooked (5-7 minutes). Blend in flour and seasonings, stirring well. Add shrimp, 1 cup half & half, milk and cream. Simmer until thick, stirring constantly. Add sherry just before serving.
Serves 6 as a soup course.

Garnish with whole shrimp and parsley sprigs.

JOE'S FLORIDA GUMBO

1 large hen, boiled &
    deboned (reserve broth)
1 cup flour
⅔ cup oil
1½ tsp. ground red pepper
3 large onions, chopped
2 bell peppers, chopped
6 stalks celery, chopped
10-12 cloves garlic, minced
2 cans chicken broth
1 qt. water
½ jar chicken bouillon
    granules
4 tsp. Creole seasoning
⅓ bottle gumbo filé
1 Tbsp. black pepper
1 lb. chopped okra
6 lbs. shrimp, peeled
1½ qt. oysters,
    simmered in their juice
    about 6 minutes

Make a dark roux with the flour and oil, adding the red pepper in with it. When darkened add the onions, bell pepper, celery and garlic. Simmer 20 minutes. Heat together the reserved broth, cans of chicken broth, water, granules, Creole seasoning, filé, black pepper, okra, shrimp and oysters. When hot, add the roux mixture. Simmer about 20-30 minutes, adjust seasonings to taste. Simmer another 30-40 minutes. Makes about 3 gallons. This freezes well. You may also add fresh crabmeat as long as you don't intend to freeze it.

This is my dad's specialty! Jonathan will always ask his Grandpa to make it when we're going home. It's a fast gumbo to put together. Dad has been so supportive in sharing his specialties with us.

BLACK-EYED PEA SOUP

1 lb. dried black-eye peas
1½ qt. water
1½ qt. chicken broth
½ cup dry sherry
½ cup minced smoked
    ham
1 onion, chopped
1 celery stalk, minced
1 bay leaf, crushed
2 cloves garlic, minced
Salt and pepper to taste

Wash beans and soak overnight in water. Combine broth, sherry and ham in a large, heavy pan. Bring to a boil; add onion, celery, bay leaf and garlic, boil for about 15 minutes. Drain peas, add to soup and simmer for about 1 hour or until tender. Season with salt and pepper. Serve immediately.
Serves 6-8.

SAM'S SEAFOOD GUMBO

1½ cups oil, divided
5 lbs. okra, sliced ¼"
  thick
1 cup flour
2 medium onions, finely
  chopped
1½ lbs. stew meat,
  coarsely chopped
4 (8 oz) cans tomato sauce
6 quarts water
1½ cups green onions,
  finely chopped
1 cup parsley, finely
  chopped
2 medium bell peppers,
  cut in large chunks
4 bay leaves
3 stalks celery, finely
  chopped
3-3½ Tbsp. salt
1 Tbsp. liquid crab boil
5 Tbsp. Worcestershire
4 tsp. Konriko creole
  seasoning
1½ tsp. cayenne
1 Tbsp. black pepper
2 Tbsp. garlic powder
2½ tsp. thyme
2-3 cups crabmeat
5 lbs. shrimp, peeled

First, you need a very large pot (at least 12 quarts). Fry okra in ¾ cup oil until okra is no longer slimy. Remove to platter-wipe out pot. Add remaining ¾ cup oil, stir in flour and cook, stirring constantly, over medium heat until roux is golden-brown. Turn heat to low, add 2 medium onions. Stir, cover and simmer until soft, stirring once or twice. Turn heat to medium, add stew meat and cook, stirring until all the red is out. Add all remaining ingredients; stir and cook over low heat 2-3 hours. Everything cooks to pieces and gumbo is thick. If you don't like it thick, just add more water. Serve over rice.

This is the greatest and so is Sam for sharing the recipe.

 A real friend is one who helps us to think our noblest thoughts, put forth our best efforts, and be our best selves.

CAESAR SALAD WITH HOMEMADE CROUTONS

Dressing:
½ cup salad oil
2 Tbsp. olive oil
¼ cup red wine vinegar
3 large cloves garlic, cut in half
2 tsp. Worcestershire sauce
½ tsp. salt
¼ tsp. coarse grind black pepper
1 tsp. McCormick lemon-pepper

Salad:
2 medium heads romaine, torn into bite-size pieces
¾ cup shredded fresh Parmesan cheese
1½ oz crumbled blue cheese
3 cups croutons
1 egg

Croutons:
3 hamburger buns
Melted butter
Garlic salt
Garlic powder
Parmesan cheese

Dressing:
Place all ingredients in a jar; shake and refrigerate overnight.

Salad:
Sprinkle cheese over romaine in salad bowl. Add the croutons. Remove garlic from dressing. Add egg to dressing-shake well. Add to salad and toss. Adjust seasoning according to taste.

Croutons:
Cut each of the buns into 6 strips. Baste with melted butter, sprinkle with garlic salt, powder and Parmesan. Repeat on the other side of bun. Bake at 300° for 30-45 minutes or until golden brown.
Serves 8.

This dressing will keep 2 weeks. Croutons will keep quite a while in a ziploc bag.

Friendship happens in that special moment when someone reaches out to another.

CAPTAIN'S SALAD

1 head romaine
1 bunch spinach
½ cup sliced purple onion rings
3 Tbsp. toasted sesame seeds
1 tsp. salt
¼ tsp. pepper
½ tsp. dry mustard
3 Tbsp. vinegar
1 Tbsp. honey
½ cup oil
3 tomatoes, cut in wedges
2 cups croutons (use the ones in the Caesar salad)

Trim and wash greens. Drain and tear in bite-size pieces. Add onion and sesame seeds; toss and refrigerate until serving. Make dressing by combining salt, pepper and mustard in a small bowl; stir in vinegar and honey. Beat with a mixer, slowly add oil with mixer running. Refrigerate. Just before serving, combine greens, tomatoes, dressing and croutons. Toss lightly. Serve immediately from chilled salad bowl.
Serves 8-10.

SPECIAL SALAD

3 avocados
2 cups sliced mushrooms
1 small purple onion
6 cherry tomatoes
Butter lettuce
McCormick lemon pepper

Dressing:
½ cup oil
½ cup white wine
4 Tbsp. red wine vinegar
2 Tbsp. minced parsley
1 tsp. sugar
½ tsp. basil
¼ tsp. thyme
½ tsp. seasoned salt
¼ tsp. garlic powder
¼ tsp. seasoned pepper
2 Tbsp. Italian dressing

Slice avocados and sprinkle liberally with lemon-pepper. Slice purple onion and separate into rings. Cut cherry tomatoes into fourths. Wash and dry lettuce. Mix dressing ingredients well. Lay vegetables (except lettuce) in a pyrex dish. Pour dressing over and marinate at least 3 hours. When ready to serve, place lettuce on a salad plate, arrange marinated vegetables on top. Spoon a little dressing over all.
Serves 6-8.

Doug says this is like a salad you'd find at a very nice restaurant.

ROMAINE SALAD

8 cups torn romaine
  lettuce
¼ cup salad oil
¾ cup sour cream
½ tsp. salt
¼ tsp. pepper
½ tsp. garlic powder
⅛ tsp. onion salt
Panola sauce to taste
1 tsp. red wine vinegar
1 tsp. fresh lemon juice
½ cup freshly grated
  Parmesan
2 cups croutons (use the
  recipe with the Caesar
  Salad)

Refrigerate romaine until crisp. Combine oil and sour cream in a mixing bowl. Add salt, pepper, garlic powder, onion salt and Panola sauce to taste. Combine vinegar and lemon juice; gradually stir into the sour cream mixture. Stir in half the Parmesan cheese, let stand 1 hour. Place greens in a salad bowl with remaining Parmesan cheese. Toss lightly with salad dressing until greens are coated. Add croutons, toss lightly. Serve immediately. Serves 6.

SPICY SPINACH SALAD

4-6 cups washed and torn
  spinach leaves
4-6 slices bacon, crisp
  fried and crumbled
½ lb. sliced fresh
  mushrooms
Mustard Dressing (recipe
  follows)
1½ cups croutons

Dressing:
2 Tbsp. dry mustard
¼ cup oil
1 egg
2 Tbsp. lemon juice
1 Tbsp. Parmesan cheese
1 tsp. sugar
1 tsp. Worcestershire sauce
½ tsp. salt
¼ tsp. pepper

Mix together the spinach, bacon and mushrooms. Pour dressing over and toss well. Add croutons and toss lightly.
Serves 4-6.

Dressing:
Mix together well by using a whisk. Pour over spinach salad. Add croutons. Toss lightly. Serve immediately.

ORANGE ALMOND SALAD

2 heads romaine lettuce
2 cans mandarin oranges,
  drained
1 bunch green onions,
  chopped
5 oz package slivered
  almonds, toasted
Dressing (recipe follows)

Dressing:
¾ cup sugar
1 tsp. dry mustard
1 tsp. salt
⅓ cup cider vinegar
1 cup oil
1½ Tbsp. poppy seeds

Chill oranges. Tear lettuce into bite-size pieces and place in a salad bowl. Add oranges, onions and almonds. Pour dressing over and toss well.

Dressing:
Combine sugar, mustard, salt and vinegar in blender. With blender running, slowly add oil. Add poppy seeds. This is enough dressing for 2 salads.

This has become our favorite salad. Even my dad thinks it's a hit!

FRESH FRUIT SALAD

1 Cantaloupe, in balls or
  cubes
1 Honeydew melon, in balls
  or cubes
¼ of a watermelon, in
  balls or cubes
3-4 Granny Smith apples,
  cubed
3-4 fresh peaches, cubed
1 pineapple, cubed
2-3 cups green grapes, cut
  in half
1-2 pts. strawberries, cut in
  half
Bananas, sliced

I use my large (Fix n Mix) Tupperware bowl with lid. Layer the fruits in order given except for bananas. (You can use whatever fruits you like). I add the bananas individually as they turn dark fast. This is a salad that keeps several days. My kids will come in and get a bowl at different times of the day. They like it without dressing but Sam and I like it with the Poppy Seed Dressing which follows.

POPPY SEED DRESSING

1¼ cups sugar
1½ tsp. salt
½ cup wine vinegar
1½ tsp. dry mustard
2 Tbsp. onion juice
2 Tbsp. poppy seeds
1½ cups salad oil, slightly
  warmed

Place all ingredients except poppy seeds and oil in blender. Blend a few seconds. Without stopping motor, add poppy seeds and very slowly add oil. Keeps indefinitely in refrigerator. May separate; if so, beat until mixed. Makes approx. 3 cups.

ORANGE FRUIT SALAD

1 medium size can crushed
  pineapple, drained
1 can madarin oranges,
  drained
1 lb. small curd cottage
  cheese
1 (12 oz) container Cool
  Whip
1 large package orange jello
½ cup chopped pecans

Mix cottage cheese and Cool Whip; sprinkle on jello. Add fruits and pecans. Let stand overnight.

Another good recipe from Aunt Loreta.

APRICOT SALAD

2 (3 oz) packages orange
  jello
2 cups boiling water
#2 can apricots, drained,
  reserve juice
#2 can crushed pineapple,
  drain, reserve juice
Miniature marshmallows
½ cup sugar
2 Tbsp. flour
½ cup apricot juice
½ cup pineapple juice
1 egg, beaten
2 Tbsp. butter
1 (12 oz) Large container
  Cool Whip
1-1½ cups grated Cheddar
  cheese

Dissolve jello in boiling water. Mash apricots and add to jello mixture with crushed pineapple and ½ the reserved juices. Cover the top with marshmallows and refrigerate until set. Mix together in a saucepan the sugar, flour, remaining juices, egg and butter. Cook until thick. Cool. Spread over set jello. Spread with Cool whip and sprinkle with cheese. Refrigerate.

Betty Jo made this for gourmet one night. It's been a hit with everyone since!

FESTIVE ORANGE SALAD

1 (6 oz.)pkg. orange jello
1 (1 lb. 4 oz) can crushed
  pineapple, drained
2 cups shredded raw
  carrots

Mix jello according to directions on package. Chill until slightly thickened. Fold in pineapple and carrots. Pour into 1½ quart ring mold. Chill until firm. Unmold on a bed of lettuce. Serves 4.

This is great in the summertime-very refreshing.

CRANBERRY SALAD

2 cups raw cranberries
1 orange, peeled, and
   divided into segments
1 cup miniature
   marshmallows
1 small can crushed
   pineapple
½ cup sugar
1 cup chopped nuts
1 package raspberry jello
1½ cups boiling water

Grind cranberries and chop marshmallows. Prepare jello and chill until slightly set. Add remaining ingredients and refrigerate until firm. Can be served as is or with cream cheese or mayonnaise on top.

SPICED PEACH SALAD

2 (3 oz) pkgs. orange jello
½ cup sugar
¼ tsp. ground cloves
1 tsp. cinnamon
2 cups boiling water
1½ cups peach syrup
1 large can sliced peaches,
   cut up
4 Tbsp. vinegar
½ cup Cool Whip
½ cup mayonnaise

Mix together jello, sugar, cloves and cinnamon. Add boiling water and stir until dissolved. Add syrup, peaches and vinegar. Mix well and refrigerate until set. Mix together Cool Whip and mayonnaise. Spread on top of set jello.
Serves 10.

SPICED PEACHES

2 (1 lb. 13 oz) cans cling
   peach halves
1½ cups sugar
1 cup cider vinegar
4 cinnamon sticks
2 tsp. whole cloves

Drain peaches, reserving syrup. Combine syrup, sugar, vinegar, cinnamon and cloves in a large saucepan. Bring to a boil, lower heat and simmer 10 minutes. Pour syrup over peaches. Let cool. Chill thoroughly. Store in refrigerator.

A nice addition for the holidays.

DEE'S SHRIMP SALAD

Boiling Shrimp:
6 lbs. medium-large
  shrimp
4 qts. water
½ cup salt
2 Tbsp. liquid crab boil
1½ Tbsp. garlic powder
1½ Tbsp. cayenne pepper
3 stalks celery or 2 tsp.
  celery salt
1 large onion, cut in 6
  pieces
1 lime, cut in half, squeeze
  juice and add lime to
  water

Salad:
Shrimp, coarsely chopped
6 hard-boiled eggs,
  coarsely chopped
1 cup chopped celery
⅓ cup chopped green
  onions

Dressing:
1 cup mayonnaise
2 Tbsp. ketchup
1 tsp. Worcestershire sauce
1 tsp. lemon juice
6 drops Tabasco

Boiling Shrimp:
Bring water and all ingredients (except shrimp) to a boil. Boil 5 minutes. Add shrimp; bring to a boil again. Boil 3 minutes; turn heat off. Cover and let set 5 minutes. Drain. Peel when cool enough to handle.

Salad:
Toss with dressing (recipe follows).

Dressing:
Mix together well.
Serves 4-6.

This is the best shrimp salad! Serve on lettuce and surround it with fresh orange segments, cantaloupe and kiwi slices. A lovely lunch.

BLUE CHEESE DRESSING

¼ lb. blue cheese
½ cup oil
1 tsp. grated lemon peel
1 cup sour cream
½ tsp. salt
1 clove minced garlic
⅛ tsp. white pepper

Combine all ingredients in blender or food processor. Chill.

DILLY ARTICHOKE SALAD

2 cups chicken broth
1 cup rice
1 (6 oz) jar marinated
   artichoke hearts, drained
   & chopped
½ cup chopped celery
⅓ cup chopped green
   onion
⅓ cup chopped bell
   pepper
⅓ cup sliced green olives
½ cup mayonnaise
¾ tsp. dill weed
½ tsp. garlic powder
½-¾ tsp. Konriko creole
   seasoning
Salt & pepper to taste

Bring chicken broth to a boil; add rice and cook, covered, 20 minutes or until done. Remove from heat and cool. Combine rice with remaining ingredients and chill well. Serve on lettuce leaf.

Betty Jo brought this to a tennis lucheon and then shared the recipe with us. You'll be glad she did!

ROBERTA'S SHRIMP GUMBO SALAD

3 cups cooked rice
1 tsp. sugar
½ tsp. grated lime rind
2 tsp. lime juice
¾ lb. cooked ham, diced
   (2 cups)
1 cup sliced celery
½ green pepper, diced
3 lbs. shrimp, boiled and
   peeled
10 oz pkg. okra (optional)
6 Tbsp. French dressing or
   Herb & Garlic
½ cup mayonnaise or to
   taste
1 Tbsp. chopped parsley
1 cup halved cherry
   tomatoes
Lettuce to serve salad on

Place rice in a large bowl; stir in sugar, lime and lime juice. Add ham, celery and green pepper. Cook okra and drain well. Dice shrimp; add okra (leave whole) and shrimp to rice mixture. Drizzle dressing over top and toss to mix. Chill overnight. Just before serving, stir in mayonnaise, parsley and tomatoes. Season to taste. Add more dressing if needed. Serves 8-10.

ROBERTA'S COLESLAW

Garlic
2-3 cups shredded cabbage
Salt & pepper to taste
Sour cream dressing
  (recipe follows)

Rub bowl with garlic before mixing salad in it. Pour dressing over cabbage and toss lightly. Season to taste with salt and pepper.

Dressing:
½ cup sour cream
2 Tbsp. sugar
¼ tsp. salt
⅛ tsp. celery salt
Paprika
2 Tbsp. vinegar

Add seasonings to sour cream; mix well. Stir in vinegar gradually and blend well.
Serves 6.

PASTA SALAD

12 oz package pasta of
  your choice
1 Tbsp. olive oil
4 Tbsp. Italian dressing
¼-½ lb. fresh mushrooms,
  thinly sliced
2 carrots, sliced thin
2 stalks celery, sliced
2 cups broccoli flowerets
1 small onion, chopped
8 oz mozzarella cheese,
  cubed
½ tsp. garlic powder
Salt & pepper to taste
1 Tbsp. olive oil
Juice from ½ lemon
¾ tsp. basil

Boil pasta in water with 1 tablespoon olive oil until tender. Drain and run under cold water; drain. Place in a bowl and pour 4 tablespoons Italian dressing over and toss. Set aside. Slice all vegetables and add to pasta. Add cheese and remaining ingredients. Toss well and refrigerate. If too dry, you may need to add more dressing.

Eggs
And
Cheese

SPINACH-BACON QUICHE

1 (10 oz) pkg. frozen
  chopped spinach, thawed
  and drained
8 oz Swiss cheese,
  shredded
2 Tbsp. flour
2 cups half & half
4 eggs, beaten
8 slices bacon, cooked
  and drained
3 Tbsp. bacon drippings or
  margarine
1 medium onion, chopped
2-3 green onions, finely
  chopped
Salt and pepper to taste
¼ tsp. cayenne
Freshly grated nutmeg
1 unbaked 10" pie shell

Toss cheese with flour. Saute onion in bacon drippings. Mix all ingredients, except nutmeg. Pour into pie shell and sprinkle nutmeg over top. Bake at 350° for 40-45 minutes or until set.
Serves 8.

ITALIAN SAUSAGE QUICHE

Pastry for a 10-inch pie
  shell
1 lb. Italian sausage, out of
  the casing
4 oz can sliced
  mushrooms
3 green onions, chopped
1 cup Monterey Jack
  cheese
¾ cup Cheddar cheese
¼ cup Parmesan cheese
4 eggs, beaten
1 cup milk
¼ tsp. salt
¼ tsp. pepper
¼ tsp. garlic powder

Line a 10" quiche pan with the pastry; prick bottom and sides with a fork. Bake at 425° for 6 minutes. Cool. Brown sausage with green onions, drain on paper towels. Beat together eggs and milk; add remaining ingredients. Mix well. Pour into pastry shell. Bake at 350° for 35 minutes or until set.
Serves 4-6.

Make your own sausage and then make this, you can't miss!

CHICKEN QUICHE

1 (10") pie shell
2 slices bacon, cooked
  and crumbled (reserve
  drippings)
1 medium onion, chopped
½ cup chopped bell
  pepper
¼ cup chopped
  mushrooms
1 cup Swiss cheese, grated
1 cup diced cooked
  chicken
½ cup diced cooked ham
3 eggs
1¼ cups half & half
½ tsp. salt
½ tsp. pepper
¼ tsp. cayenne
Freshly grated nutmeg

Saute onion, bell pepper and mushrooms in bacon drippings. Put cheese, onion mixture, chicken and ham into pie shell. Beat eggs lightly with milk, salt, pepper and cayenne. Pour into pie shell; sprinkle nutmeg over top and bake at 350° for 40-50 minutes or until set. Remove from oven and let set 15 minutes before cutting.
Serves 6.

My family really liked this.

MINIATURE SAUSAGE QUICHE

1 (8 oz) can refrigerated
  butterflake rolls
½ lb. hot sausage
2 eggs, beaten
1 cup cottage cheese
3 green onions, minced
¼ cup Parmesan cheese
¼ tsp. garlic powder
Salt & pepper to taste

Separate rolls into 48 sections and press into greased miniature muffin tins. Brown sausage and drain well. Spoon over dough in tins. Beat together eggs, cheeses, green onions and seasonings. Spoon over sausage. Bake at 375° for 20 minutes.

These are great for a brunch also!

T'S FETUCCINI

4 Tbsp. butter
4 Tbsp. flour
1¼ cup half & half
2 oz grated Romano
   cheese
2 oz grated Parmesan
   cheese
¼ tsp. garlic powder
¼ tsp. basil
Salt & pepper to taste
1 package refrigerated
   angel-hair pasta
1 tsp. olive oil

Melt butter in a saucepan, add flour and blend well. Immediately add half & half, stirring well. When smooth, add cheeses and spices. If sauce is too thick, add a little more half & half. Boil pasta in water with olive oil added. Do not over-cook. Toss with sauce. Sprinkle with additional Parmesan cheese if desired.

"Little Buddy" loves this fetuccini!

WELSH RAREBIT

4 cups Cheddar cheese,
   grated
1 Tbsp. butter
1 tsp. flour
1 tsp. dry mustard
1 tsp. white wine
   Worcestershire sauce
1 cup warm beer
3 eggs, beaten
⅛ tsp. red Panola sauce
Salt & white pepper to
   taste
2 Tbsp. sherry
French bread, sliced thick,
   buttered and toasted

In double boiler melt cheese with butter. Stir in flour, stirring constantly. Combine remaining ingredients, except sherry. Add to flour mixture and stir with a whisk until thick. Add sherry and serve over French bread.

This is very rich and makes a good brunch or "light" dinner entree.

 Friends make happiness happen.

LAYERED OMELET

½ lb. bacon, cooked &
   crumbled
4 oz sliced mushrooms
5-6 green onions, minced
4 oz package dried beef,
   diced
1 lb. grated Cheddar
   cheese
6 eggs
½ tsp. salt
½ tsp. pepper
¼ tsp. garlic powder
¼-½ tsp. Panola sauce

Layer bacon, mushrooms, onions, beef and cheese in a 9x9 baking dish. Beat eggs with remaining ingredients and pour over layered mixture. Bake at 350° for 20-25 minutes. Serves 6-8.

You could also add shrimp or chicken to this dish.

24 HOUR WINE AND CHEESE OMELET

1 large loaf day old french
   bread (broken in small
   pieces)
1 stick unsalted butter,
   melted
¾ lb. shredded Swiss
   cheese
½ lb. Monterey Jack
   cheese, shredded
9 thin slices ham (or
   Genoa salami), chopped
16 eggs
3¼ cups milk
½ cup dry white wine
6 large green onions, finely
   chopped
1½-2 Tbsp. Creole or
   German mustard
½ tsp. salt
½ tsp. pepper
½-1 tsp. cayenne
1½ cups sour cream
1 cup freshly grated
   Parmesan cheese

Butter 2 9x13" pans. Spread bread in bottom of pan and drizzle with butter. Sprinkle cheese and ham on next. Beat together eggs, milk, wine, onions, mustard, salt, pepper and cayenne until foamy. Pour over cheese; cover tightly with foil. Refrigerate overnight (24 hrs.) Remove from refrigerator 30 minutes before baking. Bake in preheated 325° oven for 1 hour, covered. Uncover, spread sour cream over top and sprinkle with Parmesan cheese. Bake 10 minutes.
Serves 24.

This recipe comes from my dear friend, Janie, who is a wonderful cook. Thanks, Janie, this is a winner.

BREAKFAST TACOS

¾ lb. smoked sausage,
   chopped
1 chopped onion
3 large potatoes, peeled
   and cubed
½ tsp. garlic powder
¼ tsp. paprika
Salt & pepper to taste
12 eggs
2 Tbsp. milk
3 Tbsp. butter
¾ lb. grated Cheddar
   cheese
20 flour tortillas
Picante sauce

Saute sausage and onion until wilted, add potatoes and cook until tender. Season with garlic, paprika, salt and pepper to taste. Beat eggs with milk and salt and pepper. Scramble in butter. Warm tortillas and fill with sausage mixture, eggs, cheese and picante sauce.

A wonderful Tex-Mex breakfast! This was inspired by my son, Doug, and his friend Jeremy.

POTATO-EGG SAUTE

6 slices bacon, cut into 2"
   pieces
4 Tbsp. chopped green
   onions
4 cloves garlic, minced
3 large potatoes, cooked,
   peeled & diced
½ cup grated, sharp
   Cheddar cheese
6 eggs
2 Tbsp. milk
Salt & pepper to taste

Fry bacon in large skillet until crisp. Remove and drain. Reserve drippings. Add onion, garlic and potatoes to drippings; cook over medium heat until potatoes are browned. Sprinkle with cheese. Beat eggs with milk, salt and pepper. Pour over potato mixture, stirring gently until done. Sprinkle with bacon and serve immediately.

Good with flour tortillas and picante sauce on the side.

EGGS AND GREEN ONIONS

6 large green onions, chopped
¼ bell pepper, chopped
2 cloves garlic, chopped
2-3 Tbsp. bacon drippings
2 Tbsp. margarine
8 eggs, beaten
Salt and pepper to taste

Saute onions, bell pepper and garlic in bacon drippings until tender. Add margarine and beaten eggs. Season to taste; stir until set.

Another great from "Papa Joe".

MARCHAND DE VIN SAUCE

¾ cup butter
½ cup finely chopped mushrooms
½ cup minced ham
⅓ cup finely chopped green onions
½ cup finely chopped onions
2 Tbsp. minced garlic
2 Tbsp. flour
½ tsp. salt
½ tsp. pepper
Cayenne to taste
¾ cup beef stock
½ cup red wine

Melt butter, lightly saute mushrooms, ham, green onions, onion and garlic. When onion is golden-brown, add flour, salt, pepper and cayenne. Brown well, about 7-10 minutes. Blend in stock and wine; simmer over low heat 35-45 minutes.

Toast our cheese bread, add ham or Canadian bacon, poached egg and this sauce for a wonderful brunch dish. Dee concocted this for our Gourmet group's New Orlean's Brunch.

The language of friendship is not words
but meanings.

Vegetables

GLAZED CARROTS

1 lb. carrots
1 stick butter, melted
Salt
Paprika
½ cup brown sugar or to
taste

Cook carrots, whole and unpeeled, until tender. Skin and cut into quarters, lengthwise. Dip into melted butter. Sprinkle with salt, paprika and brown sugar. Place in heavy skillet over a low fire until well glazed, basting with melted butter.
Serves 4.

Sam loves these!

GINGERED CARROTS
(Microwave)

1 lb. carrots, peeled
3 Tbsp. sugar
1 tsp. salt
½ tsp. white pepper or to
taste
½-1 tsp. powdered ginger

Cut carrots in julienne strips and place in casserole dish. Combine sugar, salt, pepper and ½ tsp. ginger. Sprinkle over carrots. Microwave for 6 minutes; taste and adjust seasonings. Micro for 2 minutes; test for doneness. Carrots should be served a little crisp. If necessary, micro for 2 minutes more. It shouldn't take more than 10 minutes. This is different but very good. You just want a light taste of ginger, though.

FRIED GREEN TOMATOES

Use mature green
tomatoes
1 egg, beaten
1 tsp. salt
½ tsp. pepper
Dash cayenne
½ cup vinegar
½ cup water
Flour for batter (approx.
1½ cups)

Slice tomatoes ⅓" thick. Mix ingredients for batter; dip tomatoes in batter and fry in hot oil.

These are different but very good.

BROCCOLI AND POTATO FRITTATA

3 large potatoes, peeled
and finely diced
2 Tbsp. oil
10 oz chopped broccoli
(fresh or frozen)
4 large green onions,
minced
4 large eggs
¼ cup grated parmesan
cheese
2 tsp. parsley, chopped
½ tsp. salt
¼ tsp. pepper
½ tsp. garlic powder
¼ tsp. Creole seasoning

In a large oven-proof skillet cook potatoes in oil over medium heat, stirring occasionally, until tender and lightly browned, about 12 minutes. Add broccoli and green onions, cover skillet, cook 3 minutes. Add seasonings and cook another 2 minutes. Preheat oven 350°. In a bowl beat eggs with cheese, and parsley. Pour over vegetable mixture in skillet, cook about 5 minutes stirring often. Smooth mixture in skillet and place in oven for 10-12 minutes until set.
Serves 4-6.

This would make a wonderful breakfast dish by adding 2 more eggs and chopped smoked sausage.

BROCCOLI-CAULIFLOWER SUPREME

1 bunch broccoli, cut into
bite-size pieces
1 head cauliflower,
separated into flowerets
½ lb. bacon, cooked &
crumbled
¼ cup slivered almonds
2 Tbsp. butter
2 Tbsp. flour
1 tsp. seasoned salt
½ tsp. white pepper
½ tsp. garlic powder
¼ tsp. cayenne
2 cups milk
¾ cup grated sharp
Cheddar cheese
1 cup buttered bread
crumbs
Paprika

Cook broccoli and cauliflower until tender. Arrange in the bottom of a 9x13 baking dish. Sprinkle with bacon and almonds. Melt butter in a saucepan, add flour and whisk for 2 minutes over medium heat. Stir in salt, pepper, garlic and cayenne. Add milk and cook over medium heat, whisking, until it thickens and begins to bubble. Add cheese, stirring until melted. Pour the sauce over the vegetables and top with bread crumbs. Sprinkle with paprika. Bake at 350° for 20-30 minutes.

Be a friend, the rest will follow.

CAULIFLOWER MOUSSE

Mousse
1 lb. cauliflower
1 Tbsp. butter
2 Tbsp. flour
Salt and pepper
½ cup milk
3 eggs, well beaten

Sauce:
1½ cups light cream
4 slices onion
4 rounds carrot
1 stalk celery, cut up
White pepper, cayenne,
   salt
1 bay leaf
6 Tbsp. butter
4 Tbsp. flour
4 Tbsp. heavy cream

Cook, drain and puree the cauliflower in food mill or blender. Melt butter, stir in flour, and milk, salt and pepper. Boil gently 5 min. and mix in cauliflower. Can be done ahead to this point. Reheat, add eggs, season again. Butter generously and fill a 4-6 cup souffle dish. Place dish in a pan with 2" water. Bake at 350° for 45 min. or until set. Unmold mousse on platter and serve with sauce. Decorate with parsley.

Sauce:
Bring cream to a boil with vegetables, bay leaf, pepper. Melt butter, stir in flour, salt, and cayenne. Strain on the cream, stir continously until mixture comes to a boil, thinning with milk if necessary. Taste for seasoning. Do ahead to this point. To serve, reheat, add heavy cream and remaining 2 Tbsp. butter, bit by bit.
Serves 6.

ITALIAN FRITTATA

3 medium tomatoes,
   chopped
1 cup chopped green
   onions
1 can artichoke hearts,
   halved
½ cup sliced black olives
12 saltine crackers,
   crushed
6 eggs
1 tsp. Italian seasoning
1 tsp. salt, ½ tsp. pepper,
   ½ tsp. garlic powder
3 Tbsp. oil
Parmesan cheese

Mix vegetables, olives and crackers together and place in a 9-inch pie plate. Beat together eggs, seasonings and oil, pour over vegetables. Sprinkle with cheese. Bake at 300° for 50-55 minutes.

GREEN VEGETABLE TORTE

4 Tbsp. butter
1 cabbage
1 onion, chopped
¾ lb. fresh mushrooms, sliced
3½ Tbsp. white wine Worcestershire sauce
1½ tsp. Konriko creole seasoning
1 pkg. frozen French-style green beans, thawed
2 (1 lb.) pkgs. fresh spinach
Nutmeg
2 eggs
8 oz sour cream
Salt & pepper to taste
Butter-tomato sauce (recipe follows)

Butter-Tomato Sauce:
3 tomatoes
1 lemon
Salt, white pepper to taste
1½ sticks butter
2 Tbsp. chopped parsley

Melt 2 tablespoons butter in an 8" cake pan and swirl all around to coat bottom and sides. Steam enough of the cabbage leaves to cover bottom, sides and top of cake pan. Saute together 2 tablespoons butter, onion, mushrooms, Worcestershire and creole seasoning. Cook until tender. Wash and remove stems from the spinach. Cook in a pan sprayed with Pam. When cooked down, sprinkle with nutmeg. Whisk together the eggs, sour cream, salt and pepper. Line the cake pan with cabbage leaves hanging over the sides so you can fold them over. Next layer spinach, mushroom-onion mixture and then green beans. Pour egg-sour cream mixture over all. Fold cabbage leaves in and cover top. (You may need to add more leaves.) Cover with buttered foil and place on a cookie sheet. Bake at 350° for 1 hour.

Butter-Tomato Sauce:
Core tomatoes and cut an x on the bottom. Dip in boiling water for 30 seconds. Remove and place immediately in cold water. Peel and squeeze out seeds, chop well. Squeeze lemon and place in pan with same amount of water-bring to a boil. Add salt and white pepper. Remove from heat, whisk in butter until melted. Add tomatoes and parsley.
To serve: Go around sides of pan with a knife, invert onto a plate, slice into wedges and surround with sauce.
Serves 8-10.

This was one of Bev's French creations that the three of us worked up and simplified. It's a beautiful dish. Great for a lucheon!

SAUTEED CELERY WITH PECANS

1 bunch celery
4 Tbsp. butter
½ cup boiling water
½ cup chopped pecans
2 chicken bouillon cubes

Cut celery diagonally into 1" pieces. Saute pecans in butter, remove to bowl. Saute celery in same butter, stirring occasionally. Dissolve bouillon cubes in water. After celery has been sauteed (8 minutes), stir in bouillon mixture. Serve immediately with pecans on top. No salt or pepper is needed.
Serves 4.

SAUTEED CHERRY TOMATOES

3 Tbsp. unsalted butter
3 Tbsp. light brown sugar
½ tsp. dried oregano
2 small onions, sliced (or can of whole onions)
4 cups cherry tomatoes
½ tsp. salt
¼ tsp. pepper
¼ cup minced parsley

Melt butter, add brown sugar and oregano; mix well. Increase heat, add onions and tomatoes, cook 3 minutes, shaking pan. Do not overcook. remove from heat, add salt and pepper. Transfer to serving bowl and sprinkle with parsley.
Serves 6.

GINGERED CUCUMBER SLICES

3 large unpared cucumbers, thinly sliced
1 cup green onion strips
1¼ cups white vinegar
⅓ cup water
¼ cup sugar
2 Tbsp. fresh ginger root, thinly sliced
1 tsp. salt
¼ tsp. pepper

Mix all ingredients together and refrigerate until ready to serve. This is best when made the day before.
Serves 10-12.

This recipe comes from sweet Judie. Thanks, Judie, it's delicious. Try it with the Indonesian Pork Kabobs found also in our cookbook. Judie shared that one with us, too.

A friend is someone who will love you
even when you're wrong.

MUSHROOM PIE

1 lb. mushrooms
2 large onions
⅓ cup butter
3 Tbsp. minced parsley
1 Tbsp. flour
1 cup whipping cream
4 Tbsp. dry sherry
1 egg yolk
1 tsp. water
8-inch pastry shell plus
   enough dough to roll into
   an 8" rectangle

Trim the mushrooms and wipe with a damp cloth; slice thinly. In a heavy skillet saute onions, minced, in butter until soft. Add mushrooms and parsley; saute until mushrooms are lightly browned. Add 1 tablespoon flour and cook over medium heat for 3 minutes. Add heated cream and cook on high, stirring, until cream is reduced by half. Reduce heat to medium, add sherry and simmer for 2 minutes. Let stand until cool. Pour filling into pastry shell and cut remaining dough into strips; arrange lattice-fashion on top. Crimp edges with a fork. Mix egg yolk with water and brush over top. Bake at 375° for 10 minutes; reduce to 350° and bake 20-30 minutes or until crust is golden-brown.
Serves 4 as a main course or 6 as a side dish.

Very rich!

GOURMET ONIONS

5 medium onions, sliced
½ tsp. sugar
½ tsp. salt
½ tsp. pepper
⅓ cup butter
½ cup dry sherry
¼ cup Parmesan cheese

Combine onions, salt, sugar and pepper; stir gently. Melt butter in a skillet; add onion mixture and cook, stirring frequently for 5-8 minutes. Stir in sherry and cook 2-3 minutes. Spoon into serving dish and sprinkle with cheese.
Serves 6.

FROSTED CAULIFLOWER

½ cup grated Cheddar
   cheese
½ cup mayonnaise
½ tsp. mustard
¼ cup minced onion
1 head cauliflower

Steam cauliflower whole. Mix mayonnaise, mustard and onion; spread on cauliflower. Cover with cheese and microwave until the cheese is melted.

ONION CASSEROLE

12 medium onions, thinly
  sliced
13¾ oz bag potato chips,
  crushed
½ lb. mild Cheddar cheese
2 cans cream of
  mushroom soup
½ can milk
⅛ tsp. cayenne

In a 9x13 buttered pan place alternate layers of onions, crushed potato chips and grated cheese. Mix soup and milk together and pour over the top. Sprinkle with cayenne and bake at 350° for 1 hour.

T'S ZUCCHINI

6 medium zucchini
¼ cup chopped purple
  onion
6 Tbsp. margarine
¾ tsp. garlic salt
¼ tsp. pepper
⅛ tsp. sugar

Coarsely shred the zucchini and mince the onion. Melt butter in a skillet. Add all ingredients, cover and cook over medium heat 8-10 minutes. Stir once after 4 minutes.

Very simple but a nice addition to any meal.

CHEESE STUFFED ZUCCHINI

6 large zucchini squash
¾ cup minced onion
1 clove garlic, minced
4 Tbsp. butter
1¼ cups Italian bread
  crumbs
Salt and pepper to taste
Dash Worcestershire
1¼ cups grated Swiss
  cheese

Topping:
Butter
Parmesan cheese
Fresh parsley, chopped

Wash and cut ends off of squash. Drop into boiling water for 10 minutes. Blanch in cold water. Slice zucchini in half, lengthwise. Scoop out pulp (discard 2 whole zucchini shells); chop zucchini. Saute onion and garlic in butter; add pulp, bread crumbs, salt and pepper, Worcestershire and grated cheese. Cook until soft. Fill shells (8), dot with butter-sprinkle with Parmesan cheese and parsley and bake at 450° for 15 minutes.
Serves 8.

This comes from our dear friend, Sheila, who is also a wonderful cook and fellow tennis player. Thanks for sharing She-she!

ITALIAN PEAS

2 (10 oz) packages frozen
   green peas
4 slices bacon
¼ cup minced onion
1 Tbsp. water
2 Tbsp. butter
¼ cup shredded lettuce
½ tsp. salt
1 tsp. chopped pimento

Cook peas according to directions. Dice bacon and cook until crisp, remove, reserve drippings. Cook onions in drippings until soft, remove, drain. Drain skillet, put water and butter in skillet; add peas and lettuce. Cook until lettuce is wilted, about 8-10 minutes. Add bacon, onion and salt. Add pimento just before serving.
Serves 4-6.

PEAS WITH SWEET BASIL

2 (10 oz) pkgs. frozen
   green peas, cooked and
   drained
1 stick margarine
¾ cup chopped green
   onions
2 tsp. sugar
1 tsp. salt
½ tsp. pepper
½ tsp. crushed basil

Saute green onions in margarine until soft; add peas and seasonings. Stir and simmer 1-2 minutes. Adjust seasonings.
Serves 8.

GREEN BEAN-ARTICHOKE BAKE

2 cans french-style green
   beans
1 can artichoke hearts, cut
   in fourths
¾ cup olive oil
1 cup Parmesan cheese
Salt, pepper to taste
½ tsp. garlic powder
1 tsp. Panola sauce
1 cup bread crumbs

Mix together the beans, artichokes, oil, cheese, seasonings and Panola sauce. Sprinkle bread crumbs on top. Bake at 350° for 30 minutes.

Shelley brought us this recipe from Slidell.

JOE'S BAKED BEANS

8 slices bacon, fried and
    crumbled, reserve
    drippings
¼ cup flour
½ tsp. crushed red pepper
1 onion, chopped
1 bell pepper, chopped
6 cloves garlic, minced
2 (28 oz) cans B & M
    baked beans
1 can Rotel chopped
    tomatoes & chiles
1¼ tsp. salt
1 tsp. pepper
1 Tbsp. Worcestershire
    sauce
3 Tbsp. honey
3 Tbsp. brown sugar

Make a roux with the bacon drippings and flour, add crushed red pepper, cook until medium brown. Add onion, bell pepper and garlic and saute until tender. Mix with remaining ingredients. Sprinkle crumbled bacon on top. Bake at 350° for 45 minutes.

This is another of my dad's spicy adventures.

BROILED GREEN BEANS

2 cans vertical packed
    green beans
½ lb. bacon
3 Tbsp. butter
3 Tbsp. red wine vinegar
½ tsp. salt
1 tsp. paprika
½ tsp. garlic powder
1 Tbsp. chopped fresh
    parsley
1 tsp. minced onion

Drain and rinse beans. Divide into bundles of about 5 beans. Cut bacon in half; wrap around beans and secure with a toothpick. Broil until bacon is done. Combine remaining ingredients and simmer until hot. Pour over cooked bean bundles.
Serves 8.

A friend can erase the passage of time with the
unexpected sound of her voice.

STEPHIE'S CREAMED PEAS

1 (10 oz) package frozen
  peas
1 cup finely shredded
  lettuce
1/4 cup sour cream
2-3 green onions, minced
Salt & pepper to taste

Cook peas as directed. (Do not overcook). Drain. Add lettuce, return to heat and cook until lettuce is wilted. Add sour cream, onions and seasonings. Toss and serve immediately. Serves 4.

CELIA'S POTATOES

8 potatoes, cooked, peeled
  and diced
1 lb. Velveeta cheese
1 cup mayonnaise
1/2 cup chopped onion
Salt, pepper to taste
1/2-1 lb. bacon, cooked &
  crumbled

Layer 1/2 of potatoes in casserole, sprinkle with salt and pepper. Spread with 1/2 of mayonnaise, half of cheese, cut in strips, 1/2 of onion and 1/2 bacon. Repeat. Bake at 350° for 30-40 minutes.
Serves 8.

Celia shared this with us during gourmet one night and we have enjoyed it many times since then. We know you will too!

BASQUE POTATOES

3 lb. red potatoes
6 Tbsp. butter
3 Tbsp. olive oil
3 large cloves garlic,
  crushed
1/2 cup chopped parsley
1/2 tsp. thyme
1 1/2 tsp. rosemary
1 1/2 tsp. paprika
Dash cayenne
1/2 tsp. salt
1/4 tsp. pepper

Scrub and dry potatoes. In a large roasting pan melt butter and add oil. Add garlic, parsley, thyme, rosemary, paprika and cayenne. Add potatoes and roll around in the seasoned butter. Season with salt and pepper. Bake at 375° for 40 minutes, basting often.

DEE'S STUFFED POTATOES

2 large baking potatoes
¼ cup sour cream
8 tsp. grated Parmesan
 cheese
4 slices bacon, cooked
 and crumbled
4 tsp. chopped green onion
Salt & pepper to taste
4-8 pats butter
Parsley flakes
Paprika

Bake potatoes at 425° for 45 minutes. Cut in half and carefully scoop out pulp. Add sour cream, 4 tsp. of the cheese, bacon and onion; mix well with a fork. Add seasonings and fill skins. Sprinkle with remaining cheese. Top with butter, parsley and paprika. Bake at 350° for 20 minutes.

FOIL-BAKED POTATOES

4 large baking potatoes
½ cup margarine
¼ cup chopped celery
l tsp. oregano
½ tsp. salt
¼ tsp. pepper
½ tsp. garlic powder
2 medium onions, sliced

Cut potatoes in half crosswise. Saute celery in margarine, stir in seasonings. Slice potatoes in ½-inch slices (do not cut all the way through). Lay each on a piece of foil. Drizzle mixture into slits, add onion, drizzle again. Close up foil and bake at 400° for 45-60 minutes. Serves 4-6.

This is good served with steak.

SOUR CREAM POTATOES

3 cups red potatoes, sliced
 in wedges with skin on
¼ cup butter
½ tsp. salt
¼ tsp. black pepper
¼ tsp. garlic powder
¾ cup sour cream
½ cup grated Cheddar
 cheese
¼ cup chopped green
 onion

Place potatoes in a buttered casserole dish, dot with butter and sprinkle with seasonings. Cover and bake at 375° 30-40 minutes. Remove from oven and mix in sour cream and cheese. Bake 10 more minutes. Remove from oven and sprinkle with green onions. Serves 6.

GERMAN POTATO PANCAKES

6 medium potatoes,
  peeled
1 small onion, grated
2-3 Tbsp. flour
2 eggs, well beaten
1 tsp. salt
1 tsp. pepper
Cooking oil
Applesauce

Grate potatoes and drain off any juice. Add onion, flour, eggs, salt and pepper—mix well. Heat oil in large skillet, about ½" deep; put tablespoons of mixture into oil, flatten and brown. Keep hot. Good served with applesauce.
Serves 4-6.

POTATO CASSEROLE

1 cup sour cream
1 can cream of mushroom
  soup
5 Tbsp. melted margarine
¾ cup sliced green onions
2 cups grated Cheddar
  cheese
2 Tbsp. half and half
3 lbs. potatoes, peeled,
  boiled and cubed
¼ tsp. garlic powder
Salt & pepper to taste

Mix sour cream, soup, margarine, green onions, 1½ cups of cheese and half and half in a lightly greased 3-qt. casserole. Gently stir in potatoes, garlic powder, salt and pepper. Top with remaining cheese. Bake at 350° for 30 minutes.
Serves 10.

ROASTED FRIES

4-6 baking potatoes
¾ cup melted butter
1 tsp. garlic powder
½ tsp. seasoned salt
1 cup bread crumbs
½ cup Parmesan cheese
½ tsp. dried parsley flakes

Add garlic and seasoned salt to the melted butter. Peel potatoes and slice lengthwise into quarters. Mix bread crumbs with cheese and parsley. Roll potatoes in butter, then crumb mixture. Roast at 350° for 45-60 minutes.
6-8 servings.

SAUTEED SPINACH

3 (10 oz) pkgs. fresh
  spinach
4 garlic cloves, mashed
3 Tbsp. olive oil
Salt and pepper to taste
½ stick butter, melted
1 Tbsp. lemon juice

Wash spinach; remove stems. Drain thoroughly. Saute spinach and garlic in oil over medium heat 5 minutes or until tender. Remove from heat and season with salt and pepper; add butter and lemon juice.
Serves 6.

Really good and so easy. Sam loves this.

SPINACH CASSEROLE

2 packages frozen chopped
  spinach
½ cup finely chopped
  onion
4 eggs
1 cup sour cream
1 cup grated Parmesan
  cheese
1 cup grated Monterey Jack
  cheese
2 Tbsp. flour
4 Tbsp. margarine, melted
Salt and pepper to taste
Dash Cayenne

Cook frozen spinach in a small amount of water with onion just until thawed. Beat eggs and mix rest of the ingredients with spinach and onions. Bake in a greased casserole at 350° for 30-35 minutes or until center is set. Do not overcook or it will separate.
Serves 6-8.

★ A sprinkling of freshly grated nutmeg on top of the casserole before baking adds a nice touch.

Quick, easy and delicious!

SPINACH PIE

9-inch unbaked pastry
  shell
1 cup Parmesan cheese
1 beaten egg
½ stick butter
2 pkg. cooked, chopped
  spinach
2 cloves garlic, minced
1 cup Hidden Valley
  Creamy Italian (fix
  according to directions)

Drain spinach well. Mix together with remaining ingredients and pour into pastry shell. Bake at 350° for 40 minutes.

SWEET POTATO CASSEROLE

3 cups cooked, mashed
  sweet potatoes
1 cup sugar
2 eggs
1 tsp. vanilla
½ tsp. cinnamon
⅓ cup milk
½ cup butter
3 cups miniature
  marshmallows
1 cup firmly packed brown
  sugar
⅓ cup flour
⅓ cup butter
1 cup chopped pecans

Combine potatoes, sugar, eggs, vanilla, cinnamon, milk and ½ cup butter. Beat until smooth. Spoon into a greased 2-quart casserole and sprinkle with marshmallows. Combine brown sugar, flour, ⅓ cup butter and pecans; sprinkle over top of casserole. Bake at 350° for 30 minutes.

MACARONI AND CHEESE BAKE

2 cups macaroni,
  uncooked
⅓ cup mayonnaise
¼ cup chopped pimento
¼ cup chopped green
  pepper
¼ cup finely chopped
  onion
1 can Cream of Mushroom
  soup
½ cup milk
1 cup shredded sharp
  cheese (add more, if
  preferred)
Salt and pepper to taste

Cook macaroni-drain. Combine next 4 ingredients. Blend soup, milk and ½ cup cheese. Stir into macaroni, add salt and pepper, and pour into casserole-top with remaining cheese. Bake uncovered at 400° for 20-25 minutes. (use 1½ qt. dish)
Serves 4-6.

LUAU RICE

½ cup butter, divided
2 cups rice
3 cups water
½ cup soy sauce
½ tsp. pepper
½ cup chopped green
onions
½ cup chopped
mushrooms

Melt ¼ cup butter in a 2-quart saucepan. Stir in rice; add water, soy sauce and pepper. Bring to boil; cover and turn heat to low. Cook for 30 minutes. Saute green onions and mushrooms in remaining ¼ cup butter just until wilted. Stir into rice just before serving.
Serves 8-10

MONTEREY RICE

2 cups uncooked rice
2 cups chicken broth
3 Tbsp. butter
4 Tbsp. picante sauce
2 tsp. garlic salt
1¼ tsp. chili powder
Salt, pepper to taste
1 can cream of mushroom
soup
3 (8 oz) cartons sour
cream
2 cups grated Monterey
Jack cheese
2 cups grated Cheddar
cheese

Combine rice, broth and butter in a saucepan; bring to a boil. Simmer on low 20 minutes. When rice is done, add picante sauce, seasonings, soup, 2 cartons of sour cream and 1½ cups of each cheese; mix well. Spoon into a greased 3-quart casserole dish. Spread remaining sour cream evenly over the top and sprinkle with the remaining cheese. Bake covered at 325° for 25 minutes.
10-12 servings.

A nice touch with Mexican food, I get tired of Spanish rice all the time.

Friendship is the relationship we all need to
help us through our other relationships.

PINEAPPLE RICE CASSEROLE

1 cup uncooked rice
1 (20 oz) can Dole
  Pineapple Tidbits,
  drained
1 cup brown sugar
1 stick butter, melted

Cook rice as usual. Place in greased casserole dish. Top with pineapple, then brown sugar and pour butter over top. Cover with foil and bake at 325° for 40-45 minutes. Garnish with pineapple rings and cherries.
Serves 6-8.

This comes from Gayle, a wonderful cook and very special friend from years ago. Gayle was forever creating new dishes in the middle of the night when she couldn't sleep. This is great with ham, pork or chicken. Thanks Gayle.

BROILED GRAPEFRUIT

6 grapefruit, cut in half
12 tsp. sugar
12 Tbsp. Chambord
  Liqueur
1 box frozen raspberries,
  thawed

Half, core and section grapefruit halves. Sprinkle 1 teaspoon sugar on each. Spread 1 tablespoon Chambord on top of each half. Broil for 2-3 minutes or until browned. Spoon 1-2 tablespoons raspberries in center of each. Serves 12.

HOT SHERRIED FRUIT

1 large can peach slices
1 can pineapple chunks
1 can apricot halves
1 can white Queen Anne
  cherries
1 stick butter
1 cup brown sugar
⅓ cup sherry

Drain fruits. Mix fruit in casserole. In pan melt butter, add brown sugar and sherry. Mix and pour over fruit. Bake at 300° for 30 minutes. Serves 8-10.

Meat

INDOOR BARBECUE BEEF

4-6 lb. chuck roast
Liquid smoke
Worcestershire sauce
Fajita seasoning with
  tenderizer
Black pepper
Onion salt
Celery salt
Garlic powder
Seasoned salt
1 bottle barbecue sauce

Rub roast with liquid smoke and Worcestershire. Season with other seasonings. Do both sides of roast. Cover and let stand in refrigerator at least 8 hours. Cook at 300° for 1 hour per pound. Uncover and drain off drippings last hour of cooking. Pour barbecue sauce over and bake the last hour.
I like to shred the meat and mix with the sauce in pan. It makes great barbecue sandwiches.

We prefer Cattlebaron's Barbecue Sauce.

MARY'S DIRTY RICE

1 lb. ground chuck
1 lb. pork sausage
Salt and pepper to taste
2 tsp. Konriko creole
  seasoning
1 large onion, finely
  chopped
1 bell pepper, finely
  chopped
¼ cup chives, dehydrated
2 Tbsp. parsley,
  dehydrated
3-4 cups cooked rice★
¼ tsp. rosemary or to
  taste

Brown ground chuck and sausage in deep pot; drain off all but ¼ cup of the grease. Add salt, pepper, Konriko, onions, bell pepper, chives and parsley and cook until vegetables are done. Add cooked rice and rosemary; cook over low heat for about 30 minutes, stirring occasionally so rice doesn't stick and to allow flavors to blend.

A favorite of everyone. Mary is always asked to bring this and there's never any left. Thanks, Mary, for sharing the recipe but you can still make it for me anytime.

★ Make sure you salt the rice enough when it is cooking so that you won't have to add much to the dirty rice.

It is chance that makes brothers, but
hearts that make friends.

MEATLOAF SUPREME

1 lb. ground pork
1 lb. ground beef
1 cup grated carrots
1 cup crushed Ritz
  crackers
1 cup sour cream
1 medium onion, chopped
  fine
1 tsp. salt
1 tsp. pepper
½ tsp. garlic powder
1 Tbsp. Hormel Bacon Bits

Mushroom Sauce:
Meatloaf drippings
2 beef bouillon cubes,
  crushed
1 can (8 oz) sliced
  mushrooms, undrained
3-4 green onions, chopped
1 cup sour cream
1 Tbsp. flour
2 Tbsp. Sherry or to taste
Salt and pepper to taste

Combine all ingredients. Press into a 9x5 loaf pan. Bake at 350° for 1-1½ hours. Let stand 10 minutes; remove from pan. Serve with Mushroom Sauce.

Mushroom Sauce:
Dissolve bouillon cubes in meatloaf drippings. Saute mushrooms and green onions in drippings; combine with sour cream, flour and Sherry. Add salt and pepper. heat just to boiling.
Serves 6.

FLANK STEAK REISER STYLE

2 flank steaks (about 2½
  lbs.)
1 stick margarine
Salt, pepper, garlic powder
  to taste
2 cans cream of
  mushroom soup
Chopped green onions,
  optional
Chopped fresh parsley,
  optional

Melt margarine in large skillet. Season meat on both sides with salt, pepper and garlic. Fry in margarine to desired degree of doneness (10-15 minutes for medium rare), medium heat. Remove meat to platter and keep warm. Add soup to drippings, stirring constantly. Add ½ can water and simmer 5 minutes. Slice meat on the diagonal in thin slices, pour a little gravy on top and sprinkle with green onions and parsley. Serve with rice and remaining gravy, buttered carrots and green peas. You've got a great meal in 30-40 minutes.
Serves 4-6.

FLANK STEAK KABOBS

3 lbs. flank steak
Lemon-pepper

Marinade:
1½ cups oil
1¼ cups soy sauce
¾ cup lemon juice
⅓ cup Worcestershire
⅓ cup prepared mustard
2 tsp. salt
1 Tbsp. coarse black
pepper
1 tsp. garlic powder
12 very small onions, cut in
half
2 large bell peppers, cut in
chunks
1 lb. mushrooms

Sprinkle flank steak with lemon-pepper and pound with mallet until ¼" thick. Cut crosswise into 1" wide strips. Lay in shallow pan and cover with marinade. Refrigerate at least 4 hours. Drain, reserve marinade, roll steaks up pinwheel fashion. On skewers, alternate steak, onion, bell pepper and mushrooms. Grill over medium coals, turning once, for 20-25 minutes or to desired degree of doneness. Baste with marinade while cooking.
Serves 8-10.

Good dish-can be made ahead.

HAMBURGER PIE

1 (9") double-crust pie shell
1 lb. hamburger meat
1 medium onion, chopped
Salt, pepper and garlic
powder to taste
1 can cream of mushroom
soup
1 (10 oz) pkg. frozen peas,
separated★

Cook hamburger until brown; add onion and seasonings. Add soup and peas; stir well. Line pan with one pie shell. Pour filling into pie shell and top with second pie shell. Bake at 425° for 30 minutes. Let stand 10 minutes before serving.

★ You can use any leftovers such as carrots, corn, broccoli, etc.

My family loves this. In fact, I always make two. This doesn't take anytime to make so you can have a fun day on the tennis courts or go shopping and still have a nice meal for your family. All you need is a salad to go along with it.

DEE'S QUESADILLAS

Butter for frying
  quesadillas
1½ lbs. ground chuck
Salt, pepper, and garlic
  powder to taste
1 pkg. Taco seasoning
½ cup water
12 flour tortillas
2-2½ cups grated
  Monterey Jack
2-2½ cups grated Cheddar
2 cans re-fried beans

Toppings:
Sour cream
Avocado
Picante sauce
Chopped green onions
Grated cheese

Brown chuck—season with salt, pepper and garlic. Add Taco seasoning and water and simmer 15 minutes. Heat re-fried beans until soft and easy to spoon. Lay 6 flour tortillas out on counter. Cover each with a layer of Jack cheese, meat, beans, Cheddar and top with a flour tortilla. Melt 1½ tsp. butter in skillet; fry quesadillas (one at a time) until golden brown on each side, adding butter as needed. Keep warm. Top with toppings of your choice; heat for a few seconds in Microwave. This is very crispy. Cut in fourths for easier handling. Very filling.

I was fooling around in the kitchen one day and came up with this. It's nice, too, if you have people that just like the basics and not all the extras. Each person can have it their own way. My family loves it!
Serves 6 as meal.

For use as a appetizer, cut into 8 pie shaped wedges.

SWISS STEAK

2 lbs. boneless round
  steak
¼ cup flour
¼ tsp. celery salt
¼ tsp. garlic powder
¼ tsp. paprika
Salt & pepper to taste
3 Tbsp. oil
1 onion, chopped
1 small jar mushroom
  slices
⅔ cup water
½ cup sour cream

Trim steak and cut into serving pieces. Pound to ¼" thickness. Combine flour and seasonings, dredge steak in flour mixture. Brown steak in hot oil over medium heat. Add onion and mushrooms, sprinkle with remaining flour mixture. Add water and bring to a boil. Turn heat to low, cover and simmer about 45-60 minutes. Turn meat occasionally. Stir in sour cream.
Serves 6-8.

SIRLOIN TIPS AND ALMOND RICE

1½ lb. fresh mushrooms,
  sliced
¼ cup melted margarine
  or butter
1 Tbsp. oil
3 lb. cubed sirloin
¾ cup beef broth
¾ cup red wine
2 Tbsp. soy sauce
2 cloves minced garlic
½ onion, minced
2 Tbsp. cornstarch
⅓ cup beef broth
½ can cream of
  mushroom soup
½ tsp. garlic powder
Salt, pepper to taste

Almond Rice:
½ cup slivered almonds
3 Tbsp. margarine
1½ cups uncooked rice
4½ cups water
Salt to taste

Saute mushrooms in 2 Tbsp. melted margarine, spoon into a casserole dish. Add remaining margarine and oil to skillet; add meat and brown. Spoon over mushrooms. Combine ¾ cup broth, wine, soy sauce, garlic and onions; add to skillet scraping bottom.

Blend cornstarch with ⅓ cup broth, stir into mixture and cook until thickened. Spoon over meat, stirring gently. Cover and bake at 275° for 1 hour. Add soup and seasonings, stirring. Bake 15 minutes longer. Serve over almond rice.

Almond Rice:
Saute almonds in margarine, add rice and stir. Add water and salt. Bring to a boil, lower heat, cover. Cook about 20-30 minutes. Stir with a fork to fluff.

PEPPERED PORK

⅓ cup Creole mustard
1 Tbsp. vegetable oil
1½ lb. pork tenderloin, cut
  across grain into ½"
  thick slices
½ cup flour
¼ cup cracked pepper
⅛ tsp. garlic salt
¼ cup dry bread crumbs
3-4 Tbsp. oil

Combine mustard and 1 Tbsp. oil. Spread generously on both sides of pork. Refrigerate at least 2 hours. Combine flour, pepper, garlic salt and bread crumbs on large plate. Dip pork into mixture, coating generously on both sides. Heat oil in a heavy skillet over medium-high heat. Add pork in batches and fry until white in the center, about 4 minutes per side.

This is a hit with all the Dormer "boys".

SKILLET STEAK

2 lbs. sirloin steak
1 Tbsp. paprika
2 cloves garlic, crushed
2 Tbsp. butter
1 cup sliced green onions
  with tops (about 6)
2 green peppers, cut in
  strips
2 large fresh tomatoes,
  diced
1 cup beef broth
¼ cup water
2 Tbsp. cornstarch
2 Tbsp. soy sauce
3 cups hot cooked rice
Salt and pepper to taste

Cut steak in strips ⅛" wide. Sprinkle with paprika and let stand while cutting vegetables. Cook steak and garlic in butter until brown-add onions and peppers. Continue cooking until wilted-add tomatoes, salt, pepper, and broth. Cover and simmer 15 minutes. Blend water with cornstarch and soy sauce. Stir into steak and cook until thickened. Serve over rice.
Serves 6.

STUFFED PORK LOIN

1 (6 oz) package long grain
  and wild rice mix
4 green onions, finely
  chopped
4 cloves garlic, minced
½ cup chopped fresh
  mushrooms
¼ cup chopped green
  pepper
2 Tbsp. butter
3 Tbsp. minced pecans
1 Tbsp. chopped fresh
  parsley
¼ tsp. salt or to taste
¼ tsp. pepper or to taste
¼ tsp. Creole seasoning
4 lb. boneless pork loin
4 slices bacon

Cook rice according to package directions. Set aside. Saute green onions, garlic, mushrooms and green pepper in butter until tender. Add rice, pecans, parsley and seasonings; stir until combined. Cut a lengthwise slit on top of the loin being careful not to cut through the bottom and sides. Spoon the stuffing into the opening. Secure back together with string. Top with the bacon slices and place in a roasting pan. Place a foil tent over the loin; bake at 325° for 1½-2 hours. Remove foil the last 30 minutes of baking. Remove from oven; let stand 5 minutes. Remove string and slice.
Serves 8-10.

 A cheerful friend is like a sunny day.

STEAK AU POIVRE

4 steaks, ¾-1" thick
2 Tbsp. oil
2 Tbsp. butter
Salt to taste
Coarsely ground black
   pepper
¼ cup brandy
1 cup whipping cream
3 Tbsp. butter
Brown gravy (recipe
   follows)

Brown Gravy:
3 Tbsp. butter
4-5 Tbsp. flour
1 cup water
1 tsp. beef granules
1 tsp. chicken granules
Sherry, 1-2 Tbsp.
Salt, pepper to taste

Generously cover both sides of steak with coarsely ground pepper and press into both sides. Cover and refrigerate 2-3 hours. Heat oil and butter in large skillet. Fry steaks on high 2-3 minutes each side for rare. Sprinkle with salt after turning. Remove from skillet. Discard fat and return steaks to skillet. Flame with brandy. Remove steaks and keep warm. Add cream to skillet and simmer 2-3 minutes, stirring to dissolve brown juices. Add brown gravy (prepare ahead) and 3 Tbsp. butter. Taste and adjust seasonings. Serve over warm steaks.

Brown Gravy:
Make roux with butter and flour over medium-high heat, stirring constantly until dark, golden brown. Add water, granules and sherry; simmer. Season to taste with salt and pepper.
Serve with new potatoes: boil new potatoes, peel. Sprinkle with salt, pepper and paprika. Toss with melted butter and oil. Put into a baking dish. Bake at 350° for 15 minutes.

INDONESIAN PORK KABOBS

1 lb. lean pork tenderloin,
   cut in ¾" cubes
1 tsp. ground caraway
   seeds
1 tsp. ground coriander
1 clove crushed garlic
½ tsp. ground red chili
   pepper
2 Tbsp. soy sauce
1 medium onion, chopped
1 Tbsp. lemon or lime juice
¼ cup peanut oil
Lime wedges

Combine all ingredients except lime wedges and marinate for 1 hour in refrigerator. Grill on skewers 10-15 minutes and serve with lime wedges. This can be served as an appetizer or the pork can be cut into larger cubes and served as a main course. This goes well with rice and Gingered Cucumbers. The recipe for the cucumbers is also in our cookbook. Try it!

Thanks, Judie, this is great!

FAJITAS

2 lbs. flank steak
2 lbs., boneless chicken breasts
1½-2 lbs. pork tenderloin
Terriyaki sauce: (recipe follows)
Salsa (recipe follows)
Guacamole (recipe follows)
Sour cream
Flour tortillas

Salsa:
1 large tomato, diced
1 onion, chopped
1 tsp. chopped cilantro
6 oz Pace picante sauce (we like the hot)
½ tsp. garlic salt

Guacamole:
4 avocados
½ lemon, squeezed
¾ tsp. garlic salt
¼ tsp. black pepper
2-3 drops Worcestershire
Dash cumin

Terriyaki Sauce:
1 large bottle soy sauce
1½ bottles water
½ tsp. ginger
¼ cup brown sugar
½ lemon, squeezed
1 tsp. garlic salt

Marinate the meats in the terriyaki sauce overnight. Grill over mesquite. Slice very thin across the grain. Serve with salsa, guacamole, sour cream and warmed flour tortillas.

Salsa:
Mix all ingredients well.

Guacamole:
Mash avocados, add remaining ingredients and mix well.

Terriyaki Sauce:
Mix all ingredients together well.

 Friends are the special people in our lives.

VEAL GOURMANDISE

6 (6 oz) slices white veal, pounded to ¼" thickness
Salt, white pepper and garlic powder
Flour
2 eggs, beaten
2 Tbsp. milk
Italian bread crumbs
6 Tbsp. butter
2 Tbsp. cooking oil
12 oz Gourmandise cheese ★
¾ cup white wine
Salt and white pepper to taste
3 Tbsp. green onion, finely chopped
3 Tbsp. fresh parsley, finely chopped
1 cup whipping cream
Whole parsley
6 slices lemon, very thin

Lightly season veal with salt, pepper and garlic. Coat with flour, dip in egg mixed with 2 Tbsp. milk, and coat with bread crumbs. (This much can be done ahead of time) Melt butter and oil in large skillet and saute veal on both sides until golden brown. Remove and place in shallow baking pan and top with slice of cheese. Place in oven just until cheese starts to melt (this could probably be done in the microwave). Meanwhile, add wine to pan drippings; stir to deglaze pan. Add green onions and parsley. Stir just until vegetables are wilted; add whipping cream, season with salt and pepper, stirring constantly. Heat–but do not let boil. Place veal on a serving platter, top with a little sauce and garnish with lemon slices and sprigs of parsley. Very pretty and very good.

★ Gourmandise cheese is not always easy to find so you might check for it ahead of time. Check with your grocer. I have not found a substitute for it as yet, though.

DIJON PORK ROAST

2 Tbsp. honey
½ cup Dijon mustard
2 Tbsp. soy sauce
2 garlic cloves, minced
¼ tsp. seasoned salt
¼ tsp. Creole seasoning
4-5 lb. boneless pork roast

Combine all ingredients except roast, and mix well. Place roast in a roasting pan and spread with the mustard mixture. Roast at 350° for 32 minutes per pound. After roasting for 1 hour, baste frequently with the pan juices.

BEEF WELLINGTON

Pastry (recipe follows)
(2) 2½-3 lb. filet of beef,
  well trimmed
3 Tbsp. butter, softened
Freshly ground pepper
½ cup Cognac
Mushroom pate (recipe
  follows)
Salt
1 egg white, lightly beaten
1 egg yolk
1 tsp. milk
Speciale Sauce or Sauce
  Madeira (recipes follow)

Make pastry in advance and refrigerate.

Preheat oven to 450°. Rub meat with butter and pepper. Roast on a rack until it reaches a temperature of 120° (about 20 minutes). Remove from oven and flame with Cognac. Reserve drippings for sauce. Cool, then refrigerate.

While meat is cooling, prepare the mushroom pate.

Divide pastry in half. Roll pastry out ¼ inch thick to completely envelope meat, overlapping bottom and ends.

Spread pastry with ½ of the chilled pate. Place filet in center and sprinkle with salt. Bring edges of pastry together and crimp. Paint with egg white and secure. Repeat. Place seam side down on baking sheet. Cut designs from pastry scraps and fasten to roll with egg white. Mix yolk with milk and brush roll completely. Let dry about 4 minutes. Refrigerate until baking time.

Preheat oven 425°. Place wellingtons on baking sheet and bake 10 minutes. Reduce heat to 375° and bake 20-23 minutes. (At 20 minutes it will be quite rare). Remove from oven and let stand 10 minutes before carving. Garnish with fresh parsley.

Serve with Speciale Sauce or Sauce Madeira.

This is especially fun if you do it with a friend. It is well worth the effort!

Within the tapestry of our souls are found
the threads of friendship.

PASTRY

4 cups flour
2 sticks unsalted butter,
   cut into pieces, at room
   temperature
6 Tbsp. shortening
1 tsp. salt
1½ tsp. lemon juice
10 Tbsp. ice water

In large bowl mix together flour, butter, short-ening and salt until mixture resembles coarse meal. Pour lemon juice and ice water over mixture and toss lightly. Gather into a ball. Wrap and refrigerate until ready to use.

MUSHROOM PATE

½ cup butter
4 green onions, minced
1 lb. fresh mushrooms
Salt, pepper & garlic
   powder

Melt butter in large skillet and saute green on-ions until translucent. Chop mushrooms very fine in food processor and add to green on-ions. Cook slowly over medium-low heat until mushrooms lose moisture and begin to look dry. Add seasonings to taste. Chill.

SPECIALE SAUCE

5 Tbsp. butter
¼ cup minced onion
¼ cup minced green onion
½ cup minced carrot
2 Tbsp. minced parsley
2 tsp. chopped, fresh
   thyme (or ½ tsp. dried)
½ bay leaf
¼ cup flour
2½ cups beef broth plus 1
   tsp. beef granules
1 cup dry, white wine
¼ tsp. pepper
2 Tbsp. catsup
2 Tbsp. butter
½ lb. fresh mushrooms,
   sliced

Melt 5 Tbsp. butter in a 1½ quart pan. Add next 6 ingredients and cook slowly until soft and brown, about 12 minutes, stirring. Re-move from heat and add flour, increase heat to medium and continue cooking until hazelnut brown. Stir in broth and wine. Bring to a boil and simmer 30-40 minutes. Add catsup, pepper and salt to taste. Saute mushrooms briefly in 2 Tbsp. butter and add to sauce just before serving.

SAUCE MADEIRA

1 stick margarine
2 Tbsp. flour
1 cup Madeira
2 cups beef broth
Salt & pepper to taste

Make a roux with the margarine and flour, add broth and Madeira. Add salt and pepper to taste. Cook on medium heat for 10 minutes.

HOMEMADE ITALIAN SAUSAGE

5-5½ lb. Boston Butt
2 Tbsp. salt
3 tsp. fennel
4 tsp. oregano
1 Tbsp. Italian Seasoning
1 Tbsp. black pepper
1½ tsp. crushed red pepper
2 Tbsp. minced garlic (soak in water)
Garlic powder
¼ cup olive oil
¼ cup Parmesan cheese

Cut the Boston Butt into chunks and then run through a meat grinder. Add the remaining ingredients and marinate for an hour. Mix well, you may need to combine with your hands. At this point you may shape into patties or insert into sausage skins (these can be bought from the grocery's meat department).

This is wonderful! Another of my dad's great creations.

HOT ITALIAN SANDWICH

Italian sausage shaped into patties
1 onion, thinly sliced
8 slices French bread, cut diagonally, ¾" thick
6 oz mozzarella cheese, sliced
2 Tbsp. margarine, softened
Prego spaghetti sauce

In a skillet over medium heat fry 4 sausage patties until done, drain. In same skillet, cook onion until tender; set aside. Remove all grease and drippings from skillet.

To assemble sandwiches, top each of 4 slices of bread with ¼ of the cheese slices, 1 sausage patty and ¼ of the onion. Cover with remaining slices of bread. Spread margarine on outside of each sandwich. Place sandwiches in skillet over medium heat. Grill sandwiches on both sides until bread begins to brown and sandwich is hot. Serve each sandwich with about ¼ cup sauce for dipping.
Serves 4.

BAKED ZITI

l large box Ziti noodles,
cooked and drained
1½ lbs. ground meat
l large onion, chopped
l large jar Ragu sauce
Salt, pepper and garlic
powder to taste
l tsp. basil
½ tsp. oregano
l container Ricotta cheese
2 cups shredded
Mozzarella cheese

Cook noodles and drain. Cook onion with meat, add Ragu sauce and seasonings. Simmer a few minutes-adjust seasoning. In a greased 9x13 casserole, layer; ½ sauce, ½ noodles, ½ Ricotta and ½ Mozzarella. Repeat layers. Bake at 350° for 30-45 minutes. Serves 4-6.

QUICK NEW ORLEANS RED BEANS 'N RICE

3 (15 oz) cans Van Camp's
New Orleans Style Red
Kidney Beans
½ can water ★
Salt and pepper to taste
1½ tsp. garlic powder
l tsp. basil
½ tsp. thyme
l large bay leaf
2 tsp. green Panola sauce
4 slices bacon, cooked
and crumbled
l large onion, chopped
l lb. smoked sausage,
sliced ¼" thick slices
2 Tbsp. flour

Combine beans, water, salt, pepper, garlic, basil, thyme, bay leaf, and Panola sauce in large pot. Bring to boil; turn heat to low and cook, stirring occasionally, for 30 mintues. Meanwhile, saute onion in bacon grease along with sausage until browned a little; add bacon and flour, stirring well. Add to beans (gives a creamy texture), stir and cook 10-15 minutes. Serve over rice.
Serves 6.

This is a very easy and quick dish and it's also very good. In New Orleans, Monday is Red Beans 'N Rice Day. At our house, it can be any day. I can be gone all day and still put a nice meal on the table. This plus a salad is all you need. All the Reiser crew love it.

★ If mixture is too thick, add a little more water.

SHERRIED MUSHROOM GRAVY
(for roast)

3 Tbsp. butter
1 tsp. beef granules
1 tsp. instant minced onion
½ tsp. garlic powder
½ cup water
1 can cream of mushroom
   soup
1 tsp. red Panola sauce
2 Tbsp. sherry
½ tsp. coarse grind black
   pepper

Melt butter in skillet; add beef granules, onion and garlic. Stir in remaining ingredients and simmer 2-3 minutes. Adjust seasonings. This is great with roast. If you have any drippings from roast, add to gravy—even better.

RAISIN SAUCE FOR HAM

¼ cup sugar
1½ tsp. dry mustard
1½ Tbsp. cornstarch
¼ tsp. salt
1½ cups water
½ cup dark corn syrup
¼ cup orange marmalade
½ cup white raisins
¼ cup cider vinegar
1 Tbsp. butter

Combine first 4 ingredients, gradually stir in next 4 ingredients. Cook until mixture comes to a boil and thickens. Remove from heat. Stir in vinegar and butter. Serve warm over ham. If possible, make the day before serving. Yields 2 cups.

This is excellent over smoked ham especially.

To make the world a friendly place, one must
show it a friendly face.

Best of Friends Two
P.O. Box 5573
Kingwood, Texas 77325

Please send me _____ copies of **Best of Friends Two** at $9.95 plus $1.50 for postage and handling per copy. Texas residents add $.61 sales tax.

Please send me _____ copies of **Best of Friends** at $9.95 plus $1.50 for postage and handling per copy. Texas residents add $.61 sales tax.

Make check payable to Best of Friends.
Enclosed is my check or money order for $ _____ .

Name _____

Address _____

City _____ State _____ Zip Code _____

Best of Friends Two
P.O. Box 5573
Kingwood, Texas 77325

Please send me _____ copies of **Best of Friends Two** at $9.95 plus $1.50 for postage and handling per copy. Texas residents add $.61 sales tax.

Please send me _____ copies of **Best of Friends** at $9.95 plus $1.50 for postage and handling per copy. Texas residents add $.61 sales tax.

Make check payable to Best of Friends.
Enclosed is my check or money order for $ _____ .

Name _____

Address _____

City _____ State _____ Zip Code _____

Best of Friends Two
P.O. Box 5573
Kingwood, Texas 77325

Please send me _____ copies of **Best of Friends Two** at $9.95 plus $1.50 for postage and handling per copy. Texas residents add $.61 sales tax.

Please send me _____ copies of **Best of Friends** at $9.95 plus $1.50 for postage and handling per copy. Texas residents add $.61 sales tax.

Make check payable to Best of Friends.
Enclosed is my check or money order for $ _____ .

Name _____

Address _____

City _____ State _____ Zip Code _____

Poultry

CHICKEN AND HAM CREPES

18 crepes (recipe follows)
Filling (recipe follows)
Mornay sauce (recipe
  follows)
1 cup grated gruyere
  cheese
¼ cup grated romano
  cheese
¼ cup grated Parmesan
  cheese

Crepes:
½ cup milk
½ cup beer or water
2 large eggs
1 cup flour
1 Tbsp. cornstarch
¼ tsp. salt
2½ Tbsp. melted butter

Filling:
3 lb. chicken, cooked and
  diced
⅔ cup waterchestnuts,
  chopped
½ lb. chopped fresh
  mushrooms, sauteed
½ lb. diced ham
⅓ cup minced green
  onions
1½ cups Mornay sauce

Place about 4 Tbsp. filling on each crepe toward one edge. Roll up and place seam side down in a greased baking pan. Continue until all crepes are used. Pour the remaining sauce not used in the filling down the center of the row of crepes. Do not cover crepes entirely. Mix the cheeses and sprinkle on top. Bake at 375° for 20-25 minutes. Garnish with parsley.

Crepes:
Combine together in a blender and blend well on high. Refrigerate at least 1 hour. Make crepes following the instructions on your crepe pan. Stack crepes between paper towels. Well-wrapped crepes can be frozen.

Filling
Combine all ingredients, using enough sauce to bind.

A smile is a curve that can set a lot of things straight.

MORNAY SAUCE

8 Tbsp. butter
8 Tbsp. flour
1½ cups chicken broth
1½ cups half & half
1 onion, cut in half
6 Tbsp. white wine
6-8 drops Tabasco
1 tsp. salt
½ tsp. white pepper
½ tsp. garlic powder
½ cup grated Romano
  cheese ★
½ cup grated Parmesan
  cheese ★
1½ cups grated gruyere
  cheese

Melt butter and blend in the flour. Cook over low heat for 2 minutes, do not brown. Combine broth and cream and gradually stir into roux, beating briskly with a whisk. Add onion in 2 pieces. Stir in wine. Add Tabasco and seasonings. Cook over low heat, stirring constantly until thick and smooth. Continue to cook for 5 minutes. Remove onion and add cheeses. Stir until melted.
★ It's much better to use freshly grated Romano and Parmesan cheeses.

This sauce is great on top of vegetables, chicken or pasta, use your imagination!

STIR-FRIED CHICKEN

6 Tbsp. oil, divided
6 tsp. soy sauce, divided
4 tsp. cornstarch
1 tsp. red Panola Sauce
3 whole boneless chicken
  breasts, skinned and cut
in 1" pieces
¾ cup chicken broth
1 tsp. ground ginger
4-5 green onions, sliced in
  ½" pieces
1 medium onion, cut in 1"
  pieces
1 tsp. garlic powder
1 lb. broccoli, cut in 1"
  pieces
½ bell pepper, cut in
  pieces
1 cup cashews
Salt and pepper to taste
Hot cooked rice

Mix 2 Tbsp. oil, 3 tsp. soy sauce, 2 tsp. cornstarch and 1 tsp. red Panola Sauce in bowl. Stir in chicken to coat. Cover and refrigerate 30 minutes.
Mix chicken broth, ginger, 3 tsp. soy sauce, and 2 tsp. cornstarch.
Heat 4 Tbsp. oil in large skillet or wok. Stir fry chicken mixture over medium heat until no longer pink; remove from skillet. Stir fry onion, garlic and bell pepper until tender. Add broccoli, stir fry until tender. Add chicken and broth. Cook, stirring constantly, until thickened. Stir in cashews. Serve with rice.
Serves 6.

For a sweeter taste, add 1 can pineapple chunks.

CHICKEN PICCATA

6 boneless chicken tenders
½ cup flour
1½ tsp. salt
½ tsp. lemon pepper
¼ tsp. garlic powder
6 Tbsp. margarine or
  butter
¼ cup lemon juice
4 Tbsp. white wine
1 lemon, thinly sliced
2 Tbsp. fresh parsley,
  minced

Flatten tenders between sheets of wax paper to ¼" thickness. Combine flour, salt, lemon pepper and garlic powder; dredge chicken in mixture. Melt butter in a large skillet over medium heat; add chicken and cook 3-4 minutes each side. Drain on paper towels and keep warm. Add lemon juice, wine, and slices to pan drippings; heat stirring well. Pour over chicken and sprinkle with chopped parsley.

This is very good if you use fresh turkey tenderloin.

ARTICHOKE CHICKEN

2 (14 oz) cans artichoke
  hearts
½ lb. fresh mushrooms
8-10 chicken breasts
1 cup herb stuffing mix
2 cans cream of chicken
  soup
½ cup white wine
¼ tsp. Creole seasoning
Salt & pepper to taste
4 Tbsp. butter

Chop artichokes and mushrooms. Flatten out chicken breasts. Place mushrooms and artichokes in the bottom of a casserole dish. Mix together the soup, wine and seasonings; pour over the vegetables. Push chicken breasts partially into mixture. Cover with the stuffing and dot with butter. Bake at 350° for 25-35 minutes.
Serves 8.

CHICKEN TERRI'

4 boneless chicken breasts
½ stick butter
3 tsp. Brandy
2 tsp. minced green onions
1 tsp. minced garlic
¼ lb. sliced mushrooms
½ cup heavy cream
2 Tbsp. Dijon mustard
2 tsp. minced parsley
Salt, pepper to taste

Saute chicken in butter until done. Add Brandy and ignite, shaking pan until flames die out. Transfer chicken to platter, keep warm. Add green onions and garlic, saute 1 minute. Add mushrooms and saute 3 minutes. Add cream and reduce heat, stir until thick. Stir in mustard, parsley, salt and pepper. Pour over chicken.
Serves 4.

MOCK VEAL PARMIGIANA

1-1½ lbs. turkey tenderloin,
  sliced thin
1 egg
½ cup milk
1 cup flour
2 Tbsp. Parmesan cheese
Salt, pepper to taste
1 jar (32 oz) Prego
  spaghetti sauce
2 Tbsp. minced onion
2 Tbsp. minced celery
1 tsp. minced garlic
12 oz spaghetti or linguini
1 tsp. olive oil
2 Tbsp. butter
2 Tbsp. Parmesan cheese
Oil for frying
1½ cups grated Mozzarella
  cheese

Beat egg and milk together and add turkey slices; soak for 30 minutes. Combine flour, 2 Tbsp. Parmesan cheese, salt and pepper and coat the turkey slices. Heat spaghetti sauce and add the onion, celery and minced garlic, simmer about 20 minutes. Heat oil over medium-high heat and fry the turkey slices until done, drain well. Cook spaghetti as directed, adding olive oil to the water. When done, toss with the 2 Tbsp. butter and Parmesan cheese. Salt and pepper to taste.

To assemble: In individual oven-proof dishes layer the spaghetti, sauce, turkey, sauce and top with Mozzarella cheese. (May add additional Parmesan cheese also). Heat in a 350° oven until cheese melts.

My dad found the revelation of using fresh turkey tenderloin in the place of veal. In this dish you can't tell the difference. It's much cheaper and better for you. What a find!

MEXICAN CHICKEN SAUTE

4 oz margarine
4 oz butter
2 cloves garlic
2 medium tomatoes,
  chopped
1 large onion, chopped
2 Pablano peppers, sliced
1-3 Jalapeno peppers, sliced
½ lb. fresh mushrooms,
  sliced
2 large boneless chicken
  breasts
Salt & pepper to taste
2 Tbsp. white wine

Melt butter and margarine in large skillet. Add chicken and cook till ¾ done. Add vegetables, seasonings and wine. Simmer on low heat for 10-15 minutes.

This is good served with a rice dish.

FESTIVE CHICKEN

1 package (10 oz) frozen
asparagus
2 chicken breasts, halved
4 Tbsp. flour
3 Tbsp. oil
3 Tbsp. margarine
½ cup white wine
¼ cup bleu cheese
1 can cream of chicken
soup
Salt, pepper and garlic
powder

Thaw asparagus. Lightly season chicken with salt, pepper and garlic; coat with flour and brown on all sides in oil and margarine. Remove chicken and deglaze pan with white wine. Add bleu cheese and soup. Season to taste and pour into shallow casserole. Place chicken on top and spoon some sauce over it. Bake at 375° for 30 minutes. Separate asparagus into individual stalks. Remove casserole from oven and arrange asparagus between chicken pieces. Spoon some sauce over the chicken and asparagus. Cover tightly and bake an additional 30 minutes. Very good. Serves 4.

CHICKEN KIEV

6 whole chicken breasts (3
lbs.), skinned and boned

Lemon Butter:
1½ cups soft margarine
¼ tsp. garlic powder
1½ Tbsp. parsley flakes
1½ Tbsp. lemon juice
¼ tsp. cayenne
1½ tsp. lemon-pepper
3 Tbsp. green onion, finely
chopped

Batter:
Flour
2 eggs, beaten
Italian bread crumbs

Place chicken between waxed paper; pound to flatten-lightly sprinkle with salt and pepper. Combine all ingredients for lemon butter. Take ¾ cup of lemon butter and form into 6 sticks. Freeze firm. Place 1 stick on each breast. Roll up; secure with toothpicks. Coat meat with flour, dip in egg, then coat with bread crumbs. Heat 4 Tbsp. lemon butter over medium heat. Cook chicken on all sides (10-15 minutes). Place in greased shallow baking pan. Bake at 400° for 20 minutes. Serve remaining butter with chicken.
Serves 6.

This lemon butter is also great on vegetables, steak or fish.

 A friend is someone to tell your secrets to.

CHICKEN IN LIME

6 chicken breast halves, skinned and boned
½ tsp. salt
½ tsp. white pepper
⅓ cup oil
1 lime, juiced
8 Tbsp. butter
⅛ tsp. garlic powder
¾ tsp. minced green onions
½ tsp. dill weed

Sprinkle chicken, both sides, with salt and pepper. Place oil in a large skillet and heat to medium; add chicken and saute until lightly browned. Turn chicken, cover and reduce heat to low. Cook 10 minutes or until done. Remove chicken and keep warm; drain off oil. In same pan, add lime juice and cook over low heat until juice begins to bubble. Add butter, stirring, until butter becomes opaque and forms a thickened sauce. Stir in garlic, green onions and dill. Spoon sauce over chicken. Serve 6.

This is such an easy dish but will impress anyone who tastes it.

CHICKEN AND BACON BUNDLES

12 whole chicken breasts, skinned & deboned
1 cup molasses
½ tsp. ground ginger
½ tsp. garlic powder
2 Tbsp. Worcestershire sauce
¼ cup soy sauce
¼ cup oil
¼ cup lemon juice
2 lbs. sliced mushrooms
20 green onions, sliced
½ cup butter, melted
½ tsp. Creole seasoning
24 slices bacon

Pound chicken to ¼" thickness; place in a shallow container and set aside. Combine molasses with ginger, garlic, Worcestershire, soy sauce, oil and lemon juice; stir well. Pour over chicken and marinate 8 hours in refrigerator. Saute mushrooms and green onions in butter, stirring constantly until liquid evaporates. Stir in Creole seasoning. For each chicken breast, lay 2 slices bacon in a crosswise pattern on a flat surface. Place a breast in the center of bacon. Top with 3 tablespoon of mushroom mixture; fold over sides and ends of chicken to make a square-shaped pouch. Pull bacon around and tie ends securely. Grill for about 45-60 minutes or until done, basting every 15 minutes with remaining marinade. Serves 12.

MONTEREY CHICKEN

6 boneless chicken
  breasts, skinned
½ cup chunky taco sauce
¼ cup Dijon mustard
2 Tbsp. lime juice
2 Tbsp. butter
½ cup sour cream
2 Tbsp. taco sauce
¼ tsp. garlic powder
1 lime, sliced into 6
  sections

Mix together in a large bowl the taco sauce, mustard and lime juice. Add chicken, coating all sides. Marinate an hour. In a large skillet, melt butter over medium heat, remove chicken from marinade and brown on all sides about 10 minutes. Add marinade, cook 5-7 minutes more or until done. Remove chicken and increase heat to high, boil 1 minute. Pour over chicken. Mix sour cream with 2 tablespoons taco sauce and garlic powder. Spoon 1 tablespoon over each chicken breast and garnish with a lime wedge.
Serves 6.

ROLLED CHICKEN BREASTS

Salt, pepper and garlic
  powder
8 large chicken breasts,
  deboned
8 slices Baby Swiss cheese
8 slices boiled ham
3 eggs
3 cups Italian bread
  crumbs
1-1½ sticks butter, melted

Sprinkle breasts with salt, pepper and garlic. Wrap cheese and then ham around each breast. Secure with toothpicks. Beat eggs; dip each breast in egg and roll in bread crumbs. In shallow baking dish, melt 1 stick of butter and add breasts. Place in 350° oven for 35 minutes, turning once during baking time. Baste often, using more butter if needed.
Serves 6-8.

Very easy, very good.

CHICKEN BREASTS IN SOUR CREAM

1 package Buddig's sliced
  beef
6 chicken breasts, skinned
  and boned
6 slices bacon
16 oz sour cream
2 cans cream of
  mushroom soup
Garlic powder
Paprika
Cayenne

Finely chop the dried beef and place in the bottom of a greased casserole dish. Wrap the chicken with bacon and lay on top of the beef. Mix the soup and sour cream with the seasonings to your taste; pour over the chicken. Bake at 275° for 2½ hours. Serve with the gravy.

This is a quick company dish. It's wonderful with the wild rice and mushroom dressing in our first cookbook.

CHICKEN TORTILLA CASSEROLE

1 dozen tortillas, cut fine
1 chicken , cooked and
  deboned
1 can cream of chicken
  soup
1 can cream of mushroom
  soup
1 cup chicken broth from
  chicken
1 can Rotel Diced
  Tomatoes and Green
  Chilies
Salt and pepper to taste
1 tsp. garlic powder
1½ tsp. chili powder
1 tsp. green Panola sauce
1 large onion, finely
  chopped
1½ cups grated Cheddar
  cheese
1½ cups grated Monterey
  Jack cheese

For sauce, combine soups, broth, tomatoes, and seasonings. In a 2 quart greased casserole, layer ½ the tortillas, ½ the chicken, ½ the sauce and half the onion and cheese. Repeat the layers with cheese on top. Bake at 350° for 1 hour.
Serves 6.

CHICKEN FLORENTINE

2 packages chopped
  spinach
6-8 boneless chicken
  breasts, flattened
1 cup mayonnaise
2 cans cream of chicken
  soup
1 tsp. lemon juice
⅛ tsp. curry
¼ tsp. garlic powder
Cayenne to taste
½ cup grated, sharp
  Cheddar cheese
½ cup breadcrumbs

Thaw spinach and squeeze all juice from it; lay in a casserole dish. Lay the chicken on top of the spinach. Mix together the mayonnaise, soup, lemon juice, curry, garlic and cayenne; pour over the chicken and spinach. Sprinkle with cheese and breadcrumbs. Bake at 350° for 1 hour, uncovered.
Serves 6-8.

Seafood

SAM'S GRILLED FISH

2-2½ lbs. fish fillets ★
Salt
Lemon-pepper
Garlic powder
1 stick margarine
Juice of 1½ limes

Season fillets. Melt margarine and add lime juice. Lay fish on aluminum foil on grill. Grill, basting with butter mixture, 15-25 minutes. Last 5 minutes, remove from foil and lay directly on grill. Turn once. This is also an excellent way to fix shrimp.

Another of Sam's great dishes. Thanks honey.

★ We use mostly bass fillets as that is what Sam normally catches but I think most any type fish will do for this. Do not put fish directly over fire. Foil is placed on the grill to the side of the coals. Fillets should be ½" thick. Watch closely. Fish is done when it flakes easily with a fork.

CAJUN TROUT

6-8 boneless trout fillets
2 cups crawfish tails or
   boiled shrimp
2 cups sliced fresh
   mushrooms
½ cup chopped green
   onions
2 sticks butter
3 Tbsp. flour
1 cup whipping cream
¾ cup white wine
½-¾ tsp. salt
½ tsp. white pepper
¼ tsp. cayenne
½ tsp. garlic powder

Melt 3 Tbsp. butter in a heavy skillet. Saute trout 2 or 3 at a time, adding more butter as necessary. Set aside in a warm oven. Saute the mushrooms and green onions, remove with a slotted spoon and set aside. Add enough butter to pan to make 3 tablespoons. Stir in the flour and make a light golden roux. Stir in the cream and wine. Add the seasonings. Add the crawfish or shrimp, mushrooms and onions and cook until heated through. Spread a layer of sauce on a platter, place the trout on top, cover with the remaining sauce.
Serves 6.

A best friend is someone to lean on.

POACHED FISH

2 lbs. fish fillets, about
  ½" thick
Cheesecloth
½ cup white wine
4 cups water
l onion, sliced thin
l Tbsp. parsley flakes
1½ tsp. salt
4 whole cloves
½ tsp. garlic powder
½ tsp. cayenne
¼ tsp. whole black
  peppercorns
2-3 small bay leaves,
  broken in half
½ tsp. dried thyme
½ lemon, sliced thin

Put all ingredients except fish in a large heavy skillet and bring to a boil over high heat. Reduce the heat and simmer 15 minutes to let flavors blend. Keeping liquid at a simmer, lower fish (wrapped in cheesecloth) into the water. Simmer for about 10 minutes or until fish flakes easily with a fork. Spoon some of the liquid over the fish, occasionally, during cooking time. Remove carefully from water using a slotted spatula or spoon. Take the fish out of the cheesecloth and place on a platter and serve with Tartar Sauce. Recipe follows. Serves 4.

Sam and Susan love this!

TARTAR SAUCE

1½ cups mayonnaise
¼ cup pickle relish
½ cup green onion, finely
  chopped
2 Tbsp. parsley flakes
1½ tsp. lemon juice
1½ tsp. Worcestershire
¼ tsp. garlic powder
2 tsp. red Panola sauce
Tabasco to taste

Mix all ingredients. Place in refrigerator for 30-45 minutes. Taste and adjust seasonings. Refrigerate several hours before serving. Great with poached, fried or grilled fish.

Reprove a friend in secret, but praise him
before others.

BEV'S ELEGANT FISH

White Wine Worcestershire
 sauce
2 large fillets (Orange
 Roughy) 1-1½ lbs.
Lemon pepper
Creole mustard
½ cup finely chopped
 mushrooms
2 green onions, finely
 chopped
⅓ cup melted butter
½ cup grated Cheddar
 cheese
¼ cup Parmesan cheese

Marinate fillets for 1 hour in Worcestershire sauce. Sprinkle with lemon pepper; spread creole mustard very lightly on fish. (Use very little-you don't want the mustard to overpower the fish.) Combine remaining ingredients and spread over fillets. Bake at 375° for 15 minutes or until done.

Our dear friend, Bev, shared this recipe with us. She has been a tremendous supporter of our first cookbook and a big help with this one. Thanks, Beverly Elise.
You should be able to use most kinds of fish fillets-we tried it with bass and it was wonderful.

ORIENTAL FISH

2 lb. fish (cut in serving
 pieces)

 Sauce:
¼ cup orange juice
¼ cup soy sauce
2 Tbsp. ketchup
2 Tbsp. oil
2 Tbsp. parsley
1 Tbsp. lemon juice
½ tsp. oregano
½ tsp. pepper
½ tsp. garlic powder

Place fish in single layer in shallow dish. Combine sauce ingredients and pour over fish. Marinate 30 minutes. Remove fish and broil, using sauce for basting. Fish is done when flakes easily with a fork.

TROUT IMPERIAL

½ lb. medium shrimp,
  boiled, peeled and
  deveined
1 lb. trout fillets
1 cup flour
½ tsp. salt
¼ tsp. pepper
¼ tsp. Creole seasoning
¼ tsp. garlic powder
¼ cup melted butter
½ cup chopped green
  onions
¼ cup flour
1½ cups milk
½ tsp. salt
Pinch white pepper
Cayenne to taste
½ cup dry white wine

Rinse trout and pat dry. Combine 1 cup flour, salt, pepper, Creole seasoning and garlic; dredge fish in mixture. Saute trout in butter until lightly browned. Drain on paper towels and set aside. Stir onion into butter, add ¼ cup flour and cook 1 minute, stirring constantly. Gradually add milk, stirring constantly over medium heat until thickened. Remove from heat and add shrimp, salt, white pepper, cayenne and white wine. Carefully place trout into sauce and heat thoroughly.
Serves 4.

ELINOR'S SALMON QUICHE

1 can (15½ oz) salmon,
  drained, flaked and
  crushed
1 cup (or more) shredded,
  sharp Cheddar cheese
¼ cup chopped green
  onion
¼ cup chopped green
  pepper
1 Tbsp. flour
1 (9") unbaked pastry shell
1½ cups milk
3 eggs, beaten
Salt, pepper and cayenne
  to taste

Combine salmon, cheese, green onion, green pepper, and flour. Toss lightly to combine. Beat together milk, eggs and seasonings, gently fold into salmon mixture. Pour into pastry shell. Bake at 350° for 45-50 minutes. Let stand 10 minutes before serving.

This comes from the mother of one of our good friends. She has become one of our strongest supporters.

SALMON PASTA

3 Tbsp. butter or
  margarine
2 Tbsp. olive oil
½ cup onion, sliced thin
½ bell pepper, sliced thin
2 stalks celery, sliced thin
3 green onions, sliced thin
2 carrots, grated
1 (15½ oz) can salmon,
  boned and shredded
½ cup sliced black olives
Salt and pepper to taste
2 cups half & half
½ tsp. white pepper
1 tsp. garlic powder or to
  taste
1 tsp. basil
½ tsp. thyme
8 oz fetuccini, cooked and
  drained
1 cup Parmesan cheese

Saute vegetables in butter and oil mixture. Add salmon, olives, seasonings, half & half and ⅔ cup Parmesan; stir until blended. Add fetuccini; adjust seasonings. Sprinkle remaining ⅓ cup Parmesan over top before serving. Serve 6-8.

This dish was created one afternoon when I needed something fast and didn't want to go to the grocery. I used things I had on hand and it turned out great! The family loved it.

JUDIE'S BAKED OYSTERS

¼ cup butter
¼ cup olive oil
⅔ cup Italian bread
  crumbs
½ tsp. salt
½ tsp. pepper
½ tsp. dried tarragon
½ tsp. dried oregano
2 Tbsp. parsley, chopped
  (or to taste)
2 Tbsp. green onion,
  chopped (or to taste)
2 tsp. minced garlic
2 pints oysters
Cayenne to taste

Melt butter and mix all ingredients together except oysters. Drain oysters and place in ramekins-cover with sauce and bake at 450° for 15-18 minutes.
Serves 4.

CRAB WITH ANGEL HAIR PASTA

1 lb. angel hair pasta
1½ sticks butter, divided
1 lb. crabmeat or ¾ lb.
    crabmeat blend ★
5-6 green onions, finely
    chopped
½ bell pepper, finely
    chopped
½ lb. fresh mushrooms,
    sliced
1 tsp. lemon-pepper
1 tsp. garlic powder
Salt and pepper to taste
Sherry or white wine
    (optional)

Stir pasta into boiling salted water; boil, stirring occasionally, for 3-5 minutes, cooked but not too soft. Drain pasta-place in bowl to keep warm; add 6 Tbsp. butter, toss well. Melt remaining 6 Tbsp. butter in large skillet. Add crabmeat, onions, bell pepper, and mushrooms; cook 2-3 minutes or until vegetables are soft. Add lemon-pepper, pasta, garlic and salt and pepper to taste. Cook for 1 minute, stirring until well mixed. Add ¼ cup white wine or 2-3 Tbsp. sherry, if preferred.

★ Crabmeat blend works great for this recipe but you don't use as much. It's much more economical, also.

CRAB CAKES

1½-2 lbs. crabmeat
3 green onions, minced
2 tsp. minced fresh parsley
¼ lemon, squeezed
2 eggs
2 Tbsp. cream
1 tsp. Worcestershire sauce
3-4 drops Tabasco
1 tsp. Dijon mustard
¾ cup bread crumbs
½ tsp. garlic powder
Salt, pepper & cayenne to
    taste

Mix together the crabmeat, onions, parsley and lemon juice. Beat eggs with cream, Worcestershire, Tabasco and mustard. Add to crab mixture along with bread crumbs. Add garlic, salt, pepper and cayenne. Mix well. Shape into patties. Dot with butter and sprinkle with paprika. Bake at 375° for 15 minutes.
Serves 8.

This also works well with the crabmeat blend.

Be true to your word, your work and
your friend.

CRAB SOUFFLE

12 slices white bread
2 cans white crabmeat
1 can shrimp
1 bunch green onions
¼ cup chopped green
    pepper
½ cup mayonnaise
¾ lb. Cheddar cheese
4 large eggs
3 cups milk
½ tsp. garlic powder
¼-½ tsp. creole seasoning
Salt & pepper to taste

Cut crust off bread and cube. Mix together the crab, shrimp, onion, green pepper and mayonnaise. Place half the bread cubes in a buttered casserole, add crab-shrimp mixture, then remaining bread cubes. Sprinkle grated cheese on top. Beat eggs, add milk and seasonings. Pour over mixture in dish and let stand overnight in the refrigerator. Bake in a 300° oven for 1½ hours.
Serves 6-8.

SHRIMP 'N PASTA

5 lbs. shrimp, unpeeled
¾ cup butter
½ cup vegetable oil
¼ cup olive oil
1 cup green onion, chopped
1 cup white onion, chopped
1½ Tbsp. garlic, minced
½ cup parsley, chopped
2 tsp. Konriko creole
    seasoning
2 tsp. salt
1 tsp. white pepper
¾ tsp. cayenne
¾ tsp. thyme
1½ tsp. black pepper
¾ tsp. oregano
¾ cup white wine
1 cup seafood stock
12 oz fettuccine, cooked
    and drained

Peel shrimp and butterfly. Place in boiling salted water for 30 seconds, drain. Combine butter and oils in large skillet on medium heat. Add onions, garlic and parsley; cook, stirring often, until onion is soft. Add seasonings, wine, stock and shrimp. Cook on low heat for 5 minutes or until shrimp is done. Toss with fettuccine.
Serves 8-10.

CAJUN SHRIMP

2 sticks butter, melted
2 sticks margarine, melted
½ cup Worcestershire
   sauce
4 Tbsp. ground black
   pepper
l tsp. ground rosemary
2 tsp. Tabasco
2 tsp. salt
3 cloves minced garlic
4 lemons, 2 juiced, 2
   sliced
5-6 lbs. shrimp in shells

In a large bowl mix together all ingredients except lemon slices and shrimp. Pour ½ cup of the sauce in the bottom of a large baking dish. Arrange layers of shrimp and lemon, leaving 1" headroom. Pour the remaining sauce over shrimp and lemon. Bake, uncovered, at 400° for 15-20 minutes, stirring occasionally to make sure shrimp are cooked through. Serve with hot French bread for dipping and lots of napkins.
Serves 8-10.

SHRIMP SAKI

2 lb. large shrimp
l cup butter
l tsp. white pepper
½ tsp. salt
¼ tsp. cayenne
½ tsp. paprika

Dipping Sauce:
½ cup butter
3 Tbsp. lemon juice

Butterfly shrimp, you may leave the tails on. Rinse and pat dry. Place, split backs down, in a large shallow dish. Melt l cup butter, add seasonings. Mix thoroughly and pour evenly over shrimp. (I like to mix ahead of time and let shrimp marinate in sauce). Bake at 400° for 6 minutes, remove from oven. Heat broiler-when quite hot, place pan about 4" from heat for 2-3 minutes or until shrimp are lightly browned and slightly crisp at edges. Meanwhile make dipping sauce.

Dipping Sauce:
Melt butter, add lemon juice and mix well. Serve on heated plates fanning out from small bowl in center with dipping sauce.

Very rich but oh, so devine! We prefer only real butter with this.

SHRIMP OR CRAWFISH FETTUCINNI

3 lbs. shrimp or crawfish, peeled
3 medium onions, chopped
3 stalks celery, chopped
2 bell peppers, chopped
1 stick margarine
¼ cup flour
3 Tbsp. parsley
1 pint half & half
1 lb. Velveeta, divided
2 Tbsp. Old El Paso jalapeno relish
Salt, pepper and garlic to taste
1 large can Parmesan cheese
1 (12 oz) pkg. thin fettucinni, cooked and drained

Saute onions, celery and bell peppers in margarine. Add flour and simmer 15 minutes, stirring often. Add parsley and shrimp or crawfish; cook 15 minutes. Add half & half, ½ lb. cubed Velveeta, relish, garlic salt and pepper to taste. Cook 30 minutes. Add to fettucinni. Put in 2 greased casserole dishes (13x9). Top with ½ lb. grated Velveeta and Parmesan cheese. Bake at 350° for 20-30 minutes. Can be frozen for up to 2 months.

Lin, a very dear friend of many years, gave us this recipe. Although we now live far apart, our friendship has stayed close. Love and kisses, Lindy!

OYSTER STUFFING

1½ loaves French bread
1½ lb. ground beef
2 dozen oysters
1 heart of celery
1 large onion
5 green onions
½ bunch parsley, chopped
1½ tsp. garlic powder
Salt and pepper to taste
Turkey liver, chopped
½ lb. butter
1 can Italian bread crumbs

Soak bread in water—squeeze water out. Chop celery, green onion and white onion. Saute in butter until tender; add ground meat and turkey liver. Cook until no longer pink. Add bread, parsley, garlic, salt and pepper. Stir and cook 10 minutes. Chop oysters and add to mixture. Cover and cook 10 minutes, then add Italian bread crumbs. Stir and cook 2 minutes, then add 1 dipper turkey broth; turn into greased pan and top with bread crumbs. Bake at 350° for 20-25 minutes.

SEAFOOD CREPES

Crepes:
1 cup milk
2 eggs
1½ Tbsp. vegetable oil
1 tsp. sugar
¼ tsp. ground nutmeg
Pinch salt
¾ cup plus 1 Tbsp. sifted
  flour

4 Tbsp. butter
¼ cup minced onions
½ cup minced green
  onions
1 tsp. salt
½ tsp. white pepper
½ tsp. cayenne
¼ tsp. dried basil
⅛ tsp. dried thyme
1 Tbsp. flour
1¼ cups heavy cream
½ lb. lump crabmeat
1 lb. peeled crawfish tails
¾ lb. peeled medium
  shrimp

Crepes:
In a medium bowl combine the milk, eggs, oil, sugar, nutmeg and salt; mix well with a whisk. Add flour and whisk again just until well blended and no lumps remain. Cook crepes as desired, brown only one side. Keep crepes covered with a damp cloth at room temperature. Use within 2 hours.
Makes 12 crepes.

Melt the butter in a saucepan over high heat. Add onions and saute 2-3 minutes. stirring. Add seasonings and cook 1 minute. Add green onions and flour, stirring until completely blended. Stir in the cream and bring to a boil, stirring. Add crabmeat, return to a boil, stirring often and try not to break up the crabmeat. Reduce heat and simmer until thick, stirring constantly. Return to high heat, add crawfish and shrimp; cook until shrimp are pink, about 3-4 minutes. Remove from heat and serve. Place 2 crepes on a plate, fill with ⅓ cup filling and fold in thirds. Spoon a little filling on top. If crawfish is not available, use 1 lb. of crabmeat and 1¼ lb. shrimp.

GREEK FRIED SHRIMP

⅓ cup olive oil
1¼ cups vegetable oil
⅓ tsp. crushed red pepper
1 tsp. Creole seasoning
½ tsp. black pepper
1 tsp. garlic salt
⅛ tsp. paprika
5 lbs. large shrimp,
  deheaded and split backs

Combine all ingredients, except shrimp, in a large skillet. On medium-high, heat grease, then add shrimp. Cook until pink on one side, turn over and cook on the other side. Peel and enjoy!

One of my dad's Saturday afternoon experiments.

MUSHROOMS POLONAISE

4 Tbsp. butter
1 clove garlic, minced
1 lb. sliced mushrooms,
   (can use canned)
3 Tbsp. finely chopped
   parsley
Salt & freshly ground
   pepper
1 Tbsp. sherry or white
   wine
1 cup sour cream

Melt butter in a chafing dish. When foaming, add garlic and mushrooms. Sprinkle with parsley, salt and pepper. Add sherry or wine. Saute, stirring frequently, until tender. Fold in sour cream.

Good over fried fish.

DORENE'S CLAM SAUCE FOR LINGUINE

2 cans (6½ oz each)
   minced clams
2 Tbsp. olive oil
2 Tbsp. butter or
   margarine
2 garlic cloves, minced
2 Tbsp. flour
¼ cup chopped parsley
¼ tsp. salt
¼ tsp. grated lemon peel
1 lb. linguine or other
   pasta, cooked
Grated Parmesan or
   romano cheese

Drain broth from clams; set aside. In saucepan, heat oil and butter or margarine. Add garlic and saute one minute. Sprinkle flour and cook, stirring constantly, one minute. Add clam broth, parsley, salt, pepper and lemon peel; simmer 10 minutes. Add clams and heat. Toss with cooked pasta. Serve with cheese.
Serves 4.

Dorene is our neat little friend who tells it like it is, we adore her!

 Happy is the house that shelters a friend.

Cakes
And
Pies

CARROT CAKE

3 cups sifted flour
2 tsp. baking powder
2 tsp. baking soda
2 tsp. cinnamon
½ tsp. salt
1 cup white raisins
1 cup chopped walnuts
2 cups sugar
1¼ cups oil
1 tsp. vanilla
4 large eggs
3 cups finely grated
  carrots
Cream cheese frosting
  (recipe follows)

Cream Cheese Frosting:
1 stick margarine
8 oz cream cheese
1 box powdered sugar
2 tsp. vanilla
½ cup chopped walnuts
  (optional)

Sift together the flour, baking powder, baking soda, cinnamon and salt. In another bowl mix together the raisins and walnuts. In a large mixing bowl, beat together the sugar, oil and vanilla. Thoroughly beat in the eggs, one at a time. Stir in sifted dry ingredients in several additions alternately with carrots, blending just until smooth. Stir in floured raisin-walnut mixture. Bake in a greased bundt pan at 350° for 1¼ hours. Place on wire rack to cool, turn right side up. Ice with cream cheese frosting.

Cream Cheese Frosting:
Have ingredients at room temperature and combine in order given. Beat well.

BLUEBERRY DREAM CAKE

1 Duncan Hines angel food
  cake mix
1 cup sugar
1 cup powdered sugar
8 oz cream cheese
2 tsp. vanilla
1 (2 pkg.) box Dream Whip
1 cup milk
1 can blueberry pie filling

Bake cake as directed, cool. Slice into 3 layers and set aside. Cream together sugar, powdered sugar, cream cheese and vanilla, set aside. Whip both packages of Dream Whip with 1 cup milk until stiff. Blend the sugar mixture and Dream Whip together until smooth and creamy. Ice cake layers and sides, then chill. Spoon blueberry pie filling over top and let drizzle down sides. You can also use strawberry or cherry pie filling.

This is a beautiful cake, very easy and very good and we thank Betty Jo for sharing it with us.

ALMOND-CRUSTED POUNDCAKE

Almond Crust:
⅓ cup butter, softened
½ cup packed light brown
  sugar
¾ cup flour
1 cup sliced almonds

Poundcake:
⅓ cup butter, softened
3 oz cream cheese,
  softened
½ cup sugar
2 eggs
1 cup flour
½ tsp. baking powder
¼ tsp. salt
1 tsp. vanilla
1 tsp. almond extract

Almond Crust:
Cream butter with sugar until fluffy. Add flour and mix until crumbly. Stir in almonds. Pat mixture evenly over bottom and partially up sides of a 4x8 loaf pan. Set aside.

Poundcake:
Cream butter, cream cheese and sugar until smooth and fluffy. Blend in eggs. Mix in flour, baking powder and salt. Stir in vanilla and almond extract. Spoon batter into crust lined pan. Bake at 350° for 45 minutes. Cool on rack. Run knife between cake and pan. Turn top side up. Slice thinly to serve.

HEATH BAR CAKE

Duncan Hines angel food
  cake mix
2 cups whipping cream
1 jar fudge topping mix
6 Heath bars, crushed

Make the cake according to package directions. Cut into 3 layers. Whip the cream until soft peaks form. Layer whipping cream, fudge topping and crushed Heath bars in between layers. Ice entire cake with remaining whipped cream, Drizzle some topping on top and sprinkle with remaining candy. Refrigerate and enjoy!

Variations: Add 2 tsp. Amaretto to whipping cream and substitute almond brickle for the Heath bars.

Betty Jo made this for us and used peanut butter brittle instead of Heath bars. It was wonderful.

7-UP CAKE

Duncan Hines pineapple
   supreme cake mix
¾ cup oil
1 package instant vanilla
   pudding
4 large eggs
1 king-size 7-up (12 oz)
Icing (recipe follows)

Icing:
1½ cups sugar
¾ stick margarine
1½ Tbsp. flour
2 eggs
1 (No. 2) can crushed
   pineapple

Combine cake mix, oil, pudding mix, eggs and 7-up well. Bake in a 9x13 inch pan for 25-30 minutes or until done. Frost. Oven 350°.

Icing:
Combine all ingredients and cook over medium heat 10 minutes or until thickened. Pour over cake.

ALMOND COOKIE CAKE

2⅔ cups flour
1⅓ cups sugar
1⅓ cups, unsalted butter
½ tsp. salt
2 eggs

Filling:
1 cup finely chopped
   almonds
½ cup sugar
1 tsp. grated lemon peel
½ cup sugar
¼ cup butter
1 Tbsp. milk
¾ cup sliced almonds

In a large bowl blend 2⅔ cups flour, 1⅓ cups sugar, 1⅓ cups butter, salt and one egg at low speed until dough forms. Divide dough in half; spread half in bottom of a greased 10" springform pan. In a small bowl, blend the finely chopped almonds, ½ cup sugar, lemon peel and one slightly beaten egg. Spread over crust to within ½ inch of sides. Between wax paper, press remaining dough to a 10" circle. Remove top layer of wax paper and place dough over filling. Remove wax paper and press dough into place. In a small saucepan combine ½ cup sugar, ¼ cup butter and 1 Tbsp. milk. Cook over low heat until sugar dissolves; stir in almonds and cool. Spread on top of dough. Bake at 325° for 55-65 minutes or until light golden brown. Cool 15 minutes, remove from pan. Cool completely.
12-18 servings.

This is another of Bev's creations.

CHOCOLATE MARSHMALLOW CAKE

2 sticks butter
4 Tbsp. cocoa
2 cups sugar
1½ cups flour
4 eggs, beaten
1 tsp. vanilla
1 cup chopped pecans
Miniature marshmallows
Icing (recipe follows)

Put butter and cocoa in a pan and bring to a boil. Sift sugar and flour. Pour butter and cocoa over flour-sugar mixture and blend. Add eggs, vanilla and pecans. Bake at 350° for 30 minutes in a greased 9x13 pan. Remove from oven and top with the marshmallows (the more-the better). Cover with foil and let the marshmallows melt. Spread icing over the marshmallows.

Icing:
1 stick butter
4 Tbsp. cocoa
6 Tbsp. evaporated milk
1 box powdered sugar
Chopped pecans for top

Icing:
Bring butter, cocoa and milk to a boil, fold in the sugar and let boil 1 minute only. Pour on cake and sprinkle with pecans.

GERMAN CHOCOLATE CAKE

4 oz package German
   sweet chocolate
½ cup boiling water
1 cup butter
2 cups sugar
4 egg yolks
1½ tsp. vanilla
2½ cups sifted cake flour
1 tsp. baking soda
½ tsp. salt
1 cup buttermilk
4 egg whites, stiffly beaten
Coconut Frosting (recipe
   follows)

Melt chocolate in boiling water, cool. Cream butter and sugar until fluffy. Add yolks, one at a time, beating well after each. Blend in vanilla and chocolate. Sift flour with soda and salt; add alternately with buttermilk to chocolate mixture, beating after each addition until smooth. Fold in beaten whites. Pour into 3 (9") layer pans, lined on bottom with paper. Bake at 350° for 30-35 minutes. Cool. Frost tops only.

Coconut Icing:
1 cup evaporated milk
1 cup sugar
3 slightly beaten egg yolks
½ cup butter
1½ tsp. vanilla
1⅓ cups flaked coconut
1½ cups chopped pecans

Coconut Icing:
Combine milk, sugar, egg yolks, butter and vanilla in a saucepan. Cook and stir over medium heat until thickened, about 12 minutes. Add coconut and pecans, stirring well. Cool until thick enough to spread, beating occasionally.

Unlike most German chocolate cakes this one is very moist. Be sure and use only cake flour, sifted. I also only use butter. This is Eddie's favorite, his birthday treat every year.

GERMAN CHOCOLATE CHEESECAKE

1 package German
   chocolate cake mix
⅔ cup shredded coconut
⅓ cup margarine, softened
3 eggs
16 oz cream cheese,
   softened
2 tsp. vanilla
¾ cup sugar
Sour cream frosting
   (recipe follows)

Sour Cream Frosting:
¼ cup sugar
1 Tbsp. vanilla
2 cups sour cream
2 tsp. Amaretto
½ bar German sweet
   chocolate
1 tsp. Amaretto

Mix cake mix, coconut, margarine and 1 egg. Place into the bottom of a 9x13 pan. Beat cream cheese with 2 eggs, vanilla and sugar until smooth. Spread over mixture in pan. Bake at 350° for 20-25 minutes. Remove from oven and spread with frosting. Let cake cool. Refrigerate at least 8 hours.

Sour Cream Frosting:
Combine sugar, vanilla, sour cream and 2 teaspoons Amaretto; stir until sugar is dissolved. Spread on cake. Melt German chocolate with 1 teaspoon Amaretto and a few drops of water if needed to make a flowable consistency. Drizzle on top. Refrigerate.

Thanks Bev for helping us work this up.

CHERRY POUNDCAKE

½ lb. butter
8 oz cream cheese
2 cups sugar
6 eggs
1 tsp. vanilla
2 cups cake flour
1 cup chopped walnuts
1 jar maraschino cherries
   (floured)

Cream butter and cream cheese until smooth. Add sugar and beat well. Add eggs, one at a time, beating after each. Add vanilla and cake flour blending well. Stir in walnuts and cherries. Pour into a greased and floured tube pan. Bake at 350° for 1 hour.

This recipe comes from a friend and big cookbook promoter, Carol. She has a shop in Houston, that has really pushed our first cookbook.

A friend is someone who puts seeing you
ahead of being seen.

PARTY-TIME CHOCOLATE CAKE

Cake:
1 Duncan Hines Devil's
Food cake mix
1 tsp. almond extract

Filling:
1 (12 oz) carton Cool whip
¾ cup finely chopped
pecans
½ tsp. almond extract

Frosting:
1 stick margarine, soft
1 box powdered sugar
¼ cup milk
2 Tbsp. Hershey's Cocoa
½ tsp. vanilla
1 tsp. almond extract

Cake:
Bake as directed on package, adding 1 tsp. almond extract to ingredients. Use 2 (9") pans.

Filling:
Combine Cool whip, pecans and almond extract.

Frosting:
Combine all ingredients in small mixing bowl. Beat on medium to high speed until creamy and desired spreading consistency.

To assemble: Split each cake layer in half. Place ⅓ of Cool whip between each layer. Frost top and sides with chocolate frosting. Swirling the top and sides gives a pretty effect. Refrigerate.

This was created for Sam's birthday one year and has been a favorite party cake ever since. Even people who aren't crazy about chocolate like it. Can be made 1-2 days ahead of time. Keep refrigerated because of the cream filling.

Easy and delicious!

CHOCOLATE CHIP POUND CAKE

1 white cake mix
1 small pkg. instant vanilla
pudding
1 small pkg. instant
chocolate pudding
½ cup oil
4 eggs
1½ cups water
1 pkg. chocolate morsels

Mix together. Pour into a greased Bundt pan and bake at 350° for 1-1¼ hours.

Quick, easy and good. Thanks again, Pam.

ORANGE GRANOLA CAKE

Granola Topping (recipe
  follows)
1 orange
1 pkg. yellow, orange,
  carrot or spice cake mix
2/3 cup orange juice
1/2 cup sour cream
1/3 cup oil
2 Tbsp. grated orange peel
3 eggs
Orange Glaze (recipe
  follows)

Granola Topping:
2 cups granola
1/2 cup packed brown
  sugar
1/3 cup melted butter
1/2 tsp. cinnamon

Orange Glaze:
1/2 cup ready to spread
  vanilla frosting
1 Tbsp. butter
1 tsp. grated orange peel

Prepare granola topping; reserve. Cut orange into 1/4-inch slices, then into halves, peel and reserve. Mix dry cake mix, orange juice, sour cream, oil, orange peel and eggs in large bowl on low speed until thoroughly blended. Beat on medium speed for 2 minutes. Pour half the batter into a greased 9x13 pan, sprinkle with half of topping. Arrange orange slices on topping. Spread remaining batter over top, then remaining topping. Bake at 350° for 35-40 minutes. Cool. Drizzle with orange glaze.

Granola Topping:
Combine all ingredients thoroughly.

Orange Glaze:
Combine in a saucepan over medium heat until desired consistency.

BETTY'S VANILLA WAFER FRUIT CAKE

12 oz box vanilla wafers
1/2 lb. candied red cherries,
  halved
1/2 lb. candied green
  pineapple, cut in small
  wedges
1 lb. pecan halves
2 eggs
1/2 cup sugar
1 small can evaporated
  milk
1/4 tsp. salt

Put crushed vanilla wafers in a large bowl. Add cherries, pineapple, and pecans. Mix well. Beat eggs in another bowl; add sugar, milk and salt. Add this to other ingredients. Mix well. Place in a greased tube pan and press firmly. Bake at 325° for 1 hour.

Mom, I bet you thought I'd forgotten about this!

ORANGE ZUCCHINI CAKE

1 cup flour
1 tsp. baking powder
½ tsp. baking soda
¼ tsp. salt
1 tsp. cinnamon
½ tsp. nutmeg
¾ cup sugar
½ cup oil
2 eggs
½ cup All-Bran cereal
1½ tsp. grated orange peel
1 tsp. vanilla
1 cup grated zucchini
½ cup chopped nuts
Cream cheese frosting
 (recipe follows)

Cream Cheese Frosting:
3 oz softened cream
 cheese
1 Tbsp. butter, softened
½ tsp. grated orange peel
1½ cups sifted powdered
 sugar
1 tsp. Grand Marnier
 (optional)

Combine flour, baking powder, soda, salt, cinnamon and nutmeg; set aside. In large mixing bowl, beat sugar, oil and eggs until well blended. Stir in cereal, peel and vanilla. Add flour mixture, zucchini and nuts. Mix well. Spread evenly in greased 10x6 glass baking dish. Bake at 325° for 35 minutes or until a wooden pick inserted in center comes out clean. Cool. Spread with frosting.

Cream Cheese Frosting:
In small mixing bowl, beat cream cheese, margarine and peel until light and fluffy. Gradually add sugar, beating until fluffy. If too thick, add a little milk. Stir in Grand Marnier.

FUDGE FROSTING

3 Tbsp. butter
3 squares unsweetened
 chocolate
3 cups sifted powdered
 sugar
⅓ cup milk
1 tsp. vanilla
⅛ tsp. salt

Melt butter and chocolate in a double boiler. Meanwhile, beat together sugar, milk, vanilla and salt. Add chocolate and butter mixture and beat until smooth.

This is a terrific frosting! Great on white, yellow or chocolate cake.

DINAH'S CHEESECAKE

Filling:
3 (8 oz) pkgs. cream
  cheese
1½ cups sugar
4 eggs
1 tsp. vanilla

Crust:
2 cups graham cracker
  crumbs★
6 Tbsp. margarine, melted

Topping:
2 cups sour cream
¼ cup sugar
1 tsp. vanilla

Place cream cheese in large bowl of mixer and cream well; add sugar, eggs and vanilla. Beat for 20 minutes at medium speed.

Mix cracker crumbs and margarine and press to bottom and sides of 10" spring form pan. Carefully pour in cheese mixture and bake at 350° for 30 minutes. Remove from oven.

Beat together sour cream, sugar and vanilla until well blended. Pour over cake and bake for 15 minutes. Allow cake to cool in open oven. Refrigerate overnight.

Dinah is an excellent cook. All her desserts are fantastic!

★ I used 1 box Zwieback toast for crust for a variation. Both are good. Use processor to make crumbs.

Recipe follows for Raspberry Glaze and Strawberry Glaze if you prefer one, but this cheesecake is excellent as it is.

RASPBERRY GLAZE

1 (12 oz) pkg. frozen
  raspberries, thawed and
  pureed in blender
¼ cup sugar
1-2 Tbsp. cornstarch
½ cup raspberry jam

Combine raspberries, sugar, 1 Tbsp. cornstarch and jam. Cook, stirring constantly, until thickened. If not thick enough, dissolve remaining cornstarch in a little water and add to sauce. Cook and stir 1 minute more. Strain and cool. Straining the sauce takes a little time but it's worth the effort if you don't like seeds. Sam doesn't!!

Another variation is to add a little orange or raspberry liqueur.

STRAWBERRY GLAZE

1 (10 oz) pkg. frozen
  strawberries, thawed
1 tsp. sugar
1 Tbsp. cornstarch
2 tsp. strawberry-flavored
  liqueur

Place strawberries in a measuring cup and add enough water to make 2 cups. Combine sugar and cornstarch in a pan; gradually add strawberry mixture, stirring until blended. Cook over low heat until thickened, stirring constantly. Stir in liqueur and chill. Spoon over cheesecake.

AMARETTO CHEESECAKE

Crust:
6 Tbsp. butter
½ package Stella D'Oro
  almond toast, finely
  ground
¼ cup chopped, sliced
  almonds
2 Tbsp. sugar

Filling:
2 lbs. Philadelphia cream
  cheese
1½ cups sugar
1½ Tbsp. Amaretto
½ tsp. vanilla extract
1 tsp. almond extract
Pinch salt
4 large eggs

Topping:
2 cups sour cream
¼ cup sugar
1 tsp. Amaretto
½ tsp. almond extract
1 cup sliced, toasted
  almonds

Melt butter over low heat. Combine butter with crumbs, almonds and sugar until well blended. Press mixture in the bottom of an ungreased 10-inch springform pan.

Filling:
Combine cream cheese and sugar in mixer, beat 2 minutes. Add Amaretto, vanilla, almond and salt, blending thoroughly. Adjust mixer speed to low and add eggs, one at a time. Mix just until each egg has been blended into the batter. Pour filling into the crust and bake at 350° for 40-45 minutes. Remove from oven and let set 10 minutes. Add topping.

Topping:
Combine topping ingredients and spread evenly over baked filling. Sprinkle with 1 cup of sliced, toasted almonds. Return to 350° oven for 10 minutes. Remove from oven and immediately place in refrigerator to cool.

This is absolutely sinful! It only took 6 tries to perfect it, but we didn't mind having to eat it at all.

This has become Dee's birthday surprise, it's her favorite dessert. She won't ever make it, it's my treat to her.

GWEN'S LEMON FRUIT CAKE

1 lb. butter
2¼ cups sugar
6 large eggs
4 cups flour
1 tsp. baking powder
4 tsp. lemon extract
1 Tbsp. butter extract
2 Tbsp. bourbon
12 oz green & red cherries
12 oz green & red
  pineapple
½ cup white raisins
6 cups chopped pecans

Cream together butter, sugar and eggs. Add flour, baking powder, extracts and bourbon. Dredge fruit in part of flour. Add fruit and pecans to mixture, stirring well. Bake in greased mini-loaf pans. Bake at 250° for 1½ hours. (Test for doneness)
Makes 8 loaves.

This is excellent for those of us who don't care for fruit cake. It makes a great holiday gift!

PEACH CAKE

1 butter recipe cake mix
1 box fluffy white frosting
  mix
1 cup whipping cream
2 cups diced fresh peaches

Bake cake as directed in 2 (9") layers. Cool and split layers. Mix frosting as directed. Whip cream and fold into the frosting. Stir in peaches. Ice layers. Refrigerate.

STRAWBERRY PIE

9-inch pie crust, baked
1 cup sugar
1¼ cups water
3 Tbsp. cornstarch
1 small package strawberry
  jello
1 pint fresh strawberries,
  washed and drained

Cook sugar, water and cornstarch over medium heat until thick, stirring constantly. When thickened, add jello. Place whole berries in crust and pour gelatin mixture over evenly. Chill. Serve with whipped cream or Cool Whip.

THE CHOCOLATE PIE

Crust:
3 egg whites
Pinch salt
1 tsp. vanilla
½ tsp. almond extract
1 cup sugar
1 tsp. baking powder
¾ cup minced pecans
½ cup saltine cracker
crumbs

Filling:
1 cup sugar
⅓ cup cocoa
⅓ cup flour
3 egg yolks
1¾ cups milk
1 tsp. vanilla
½ tsp. almond extract
2 Tbsp. softened butter
1 cup whipping cream,
whipped with 1 Tbsp.
powdered sugar & ½
tsp. almond ext.

Crust:
Beat egg whites, salt, vanilla and almond until soft peaks form, gradually adding sugar. Beat until stiff. Mix together baking powder, pecans and crumbs. Fold into egg white mixture. Grease a 10-inch pie plate and spread mixture to make a crust. Bake at 300° for 40 minutes.

Filling:
Mix in double boiler sugar, cocoa, flour, yolks and milk. Cook over medium heat until thick. Remove from heat, add flavorings and butter, blend well. Pour into baked shell. Cool. Top with whipped cream.
Serves 8-10.

This is for you, Judy.

JANICE'S APPLE PIE

4 tart apples, peeled and
diced
1 cup sugar
1 stick butter
1 cup flour
⅔ cup brown sugar
1 cup chopped pecans

Place apples in a greased pie plate. Sprinkle sugar over the top. Mix together the melted butter, flour, brown sugar and pecans. Sprinkle over apples. Bake at 350° for 40 minutes. Serve with ice cream or whipped cream.

Thanks, Janice!

Friendship is rare, never to be thrown away.

PUMPKIN CHIFFON PIE

1 envelope unflavored
  gelatin
¼ cup cold water
3 egg yolks, beaten
½ cup sugar
1¼ cups cooked pumpkin
½ cup milk
½ tsp. salt
½ tsp. ginger
½ tsp. cinnamon
½ tsp. nutmeg
3 egg whites
½ cup sugar
¼ cup coarsley chopped
  nuts
1 cup whipping cream
¼ tsp. ginger
1 tsp. powdered sugar
12-16 ladyfingers

Soften gelatin in cold water. Combine egg yolks, ½ cup sugar, pumpkin, milk, salt and ½ tsp. each ginger, cinnamon and nutmeg; cook in a double boiler until thick. Add gelatin and stir until dissolved. Cool. Beat egg whites until frothy and add remaining ½ cup sugar gradually, beating constantly to soft peak stage. Fold into cooled pumpkin mixture. Line a 9-inch springform pan with ladyfingers. Pour pumpkin chiffon mixture into pan. Chill. Whip cream with ginger and powdered sugar and top pie.
Serves 12-16.

BANANA SPLIT PIE

2 cups graham cracker
  crumbs
1 stick melted margarine

Mix together and place in a 9x13 pan.

2 sticks margarine,
  softened
3 cups powdered sugar
3 eggs

Beat in an electric mixer no less than 15 minutes. Spread over crust.

5 sliced bananas
2 cups sliced strawberries
1 large can crushed
  pineapple
9½ oz Cool Whip
1 cup chopped pecans

Lay bananas evenly over filling, then strawberries and crushed pineapple. Top with Cool Whip, completely covering fruit. Sprinkle pecans on top. Refrigerate overnight.

This is extremely rich!

CHOCOLATE-AMARETTO CRUNCH PIE

Crust:
12 almond macaroons
½ cup finely chopped almonds
½ cup packed light brown sugar
¼ cup flour
¼ tsp. salt
5 Tbsp. melted butter

Filling:
12 oz semi-sweet chocolate, chopped
2 eggs, separated, room temperature
3 Tbsp. Amaretto
2 Tbsp. sugar
1½ cups whipping cream
1 tsp. vanilla
1 tsp. almond extract

Crust:
Combine macaroons, almonds, sugar, flour and salt in processor or blender. With machine running, add butter and mix 20 seconds. Pat mixture onto bottom and sides of a 10-inch greased pie plate. Bake at 350° 10 minutes.

Filling:
Melt chocolate in large mixing bowl over simmering water; stir until smooth. Remove from over water. Beat in yolks with mixer, mixture may bind. Add Amaretto beating well, mixture will smooth out. Set aside. With clean beaters, beat whites with 1 tablespoon sugar until soft peaks form. Gently fold into chocolate mixture. Using clean beaters, beat whipping cream with remaining sugar, vanilla and almond extracts until soft peaks form. Fold all but ¾ cup into the chocolate mixture. Spoon filling into crust. Cover and refrigerate at least 6 hours. Just before serving place remaining whipped cream into a pastry bag and decorate top of pie.
Serves 8-10.

CHOCOLATE CHIP DELIGHT

1 cup sugar
½ cup flour
2 eggs, beaten
1 stick margarine, melted & cooled
1 cup chopped pecans
6 oz chocolate chips
1 tsp. vanilla
1 unbaked pastry shell

Mix together sugar and flour. Add remaining ingredients and mix well. Pour into pastry shell. Bake at 325° for 1 hour. Serve with whipped cream or vanilla ice cream.

LIGHT CHOCOLATE MOUSSE PIE

Crust:
1 pkg. chocolate wafers
5 Tbsp. melted margarine
2 Tbsp. sugar

Filling:
4 oz German's sweet
  chocolate
4 egg yolks
½ stick butter, softened
Dash salt
1 tsp. vanilla
4 egg whites
6 Tbsp. sugar

Topping:
½ pint whipping cream
1 Tbsp. powdered sugar
½ tsp. vanilla
Grated chocolate

Crust:
Combine all ingredients in a processor. Pat into a 10-inch pie plate. Bake at 300° for 10 minutes. Cool.

Filling:
Put chocolate in a saucepan and cover with 2 inches hot tap water. Cover and let stand 5 minutes, drain off water when chocolate is soft enough to put your finger through. Add yolks and whisk over low heat until thick. Remove from heat and add butter, salt and vanilla. Mix well. Cool. Beat egg whites, gradually adding sugar after soft peaks form. Beat until stiff. Beat 2 tablespoons of the whites into the chocolate, mixing it in well. Fold remainder of whites into chocolate. Pour into crust.

Topping:
Whip together cream, sugar and vanilla until soft peaks form. Spread on top of cooled filling. Sprinkle grated chocolate on top. Chill several hours.

This filling is also good just as a chocolate mousse. This is Doug and Jonathan's favorite dessert.

LIGHT AND EASY PUMPKIN PIE

1½ cups milk
2 pkgs. instant vanilla
  pudding
1 can pumpkin
1½ tsp. pumpkin pie spice
1 (9 oz) carton Cool Whip
1 baked 10" pie shell
¾ cup chopped roasted
  pecans

Blend milk and pudding together with mixer. Add pumpkin and spice and blend well. Fold in Cool Whip (reserve about half for top). Put in baked pie shell and top with Cool Whip and chopped roasted pecans. Chill in refrigerator. Makes 1 (10") pie.

This is a very light pie and it's yummy!

LEMON CHESS PIE

1 stick margarine (soft)
1¼ cups sugar
1 Tbsp. flour
3 eggs, unbeaten
⅓ cup lemon juice
1 tsp. grated lemon peel
1 unbaked 9" pie shell

Cream margarine and sugar; add flour and eggs, one at a time. Add lemon juice and peel; pour into pie shell. Bake at 400° for 10 minutes; reduce heat to 325° and bake 25 minutes.

I'm a lemon pie lover and this is great! Thanks, Mary Catherine.

SUSAN'S STRAWBERRY YOGURT PIE

1 graham cracker crust
1 small carton strawberry
  yogurt
1 (10 oz) package frozen
  strawberries, thawed
9½ oz container Cool
  Whip

Mix yogurt, strawberries and Cool Whip together. Pour into crust and chill.

This is a light, low calorie dessert. Thanks Susan!

FUDGE PECAN PIE

1 stick butter
2 squares unsweetened
  chocolate
1 Tbsp. cocoa
4 eggs
3 Tbsp. white corn syrup
1¼ cups sugar
¼ tsp. salt
1 tsp. vanilla
¾ cup chopped pecans

Over low heat melt the butter and chocolate, stir in cocoa. Beat eggs until light. Add syrup, sugar, salt and vanilla; beat well. Add the cooled chocolate mixture and mix thoroughly. Stir in the pecans. Pour into a (9") pastry shell. Bake at 350° for 35-45 minutes. Cool. Serve with whipped cream or vanilla ice cream on top.
Serves 6-8.

 Never injure a friend, even in jest.

Desserts Cookies & Candy

APPLE LATTICE FLAN

Pastry:
1¾ cups flour
Pinch salt
7 Tbsp. butter, cut into
 small pieces
2 Tbsp. sugar
1 egg yolk
About 3 Tbsp. ice water

Filling:
6 or 7 cooking apples
Grated peel and juice of 1
 lemon
½ cup sugar
1 tsp. ground cinnamon
⅔ cup raisins
1 egg yolk
⅓ cup minced pecans

Glaze:
⅓ cup apricot jam
1 cup sifted, powdered
 sugar
2 Tbsp. lemon juice

Pastry:
Sift flour and salt into a large bowl. Using a pastry blender or 2 knives cut in butter evenly. Lightly mix in sugar, egg yolk and enough ice water to make a dough. Press into a ball and wrap in foil. Refrigerate 1 hour.

Filling:
Peel and core apples and chop coarsely. Place in a large bowl. Mix in lemon peel and juice, sugar, cinnamon, raisins and pecans. Preheat oven to 400°. On a floured board, roll out ¾ of the dough to fit a 15½x10½ pan. Place dough in pan without stretching. Spread apple mixture over pastry shell. Roll out remaining dough, cut into thin strips and arrange over flan in a lattice pattern. Brush with egg yolk. Bake 30-40 minutes. Cool in pan.

Glaze:
To make glaze; warm jam and brush over warm pastry. Blend powdered sugar and lemon juice. Drizzle glaze over lattice.

BANANA'S FLAMBE'

8 oz can pineapple chunks
 packed in juice
½ cup butter
½ cup packed brown
 sugar
½ cup chopped pecans
¼ cup pineapple preserves
½ tsp. cinnamon
4 bananas, peeled and cut
 in 1-inch pieces
¼ cup rum or brandy
1 qt. vanilla ice cream

Drain pineapple, reserving 2 tablespoons juice. In a skillet, melt butter. Stir in pineapple chunks, 2 tablespoons juice, sugar, pecans, preserves and cinnamon. Stir constantly over medium heat until sugar dissolves. Add bananas; reduce heat to low. Simmer uncovered 5-8 minutes, turning occasionally to glaze. Heat rum or brandy in a small saucepan. Ignite and carefully pour flaming liquid over bananas. When flame subsides, serve at once over ice cream.
Makes 8 servings.

What a finale!

BLUEBERRY AMARETTO SQUARES

1¾ cups graham cracker
   crumbs
½ cup sugar
½ cup melted butter
2 eggs
¾ cup sugar
8 oz softened cream
   cheese
2½ cups milk
2 (3¾ oz) pkgs. vanilla
   instant pudding
½ cup Amaretto, divided
1¼ cups sugar
¼ cup cornstarch
5 cups frozen blueberries,
   thawed
8 oz container Cool Whip

Combine graham cracker crumbs, ½ cup sugar and melted butter. Press into a greased 13x9 inch baking dish.
Combine eggs, ¾ cup sugar, ¼ cup Amaretto and cream cheese; beat at medium speed until smooth. Spread over crust mixture. Bake at 350° for 30 minutes. Cool. Combine milk, pudding mix and ¼ cup Amaretto-beat 2 minutes. Spread over cream cheese. Cook blueberry mixture (1¼ cups sugar, cornstarch and blueberries) over medium heat until thick and spread over pudding mix. Chill thoroughly-spread Cool Whip over the top. You can substitute a can of blueberry pie filling for the blueberry mixture.

This recipe came from a neat lady we have recently gotten to know-Linda.
Thanks a bunch!

BLUEBERRY DESSERT

2 cups graham cracker
   crumbs
1 stick margarine
½ cup chopped pecans
8 oz cream cheese
½ cup powdered sugar
1 cup sugar
2 eggs
1 tsp. lemon juice
Blueberry pie filling
9½ oz Cool Whip
1 tsp. almond extract

Mix crumbs, melted margarine and pecans and press into 9x13 inch pan. Beat together the cream cheese, sugars, eggs and lemon juice; pour over crust. Bake at 350° for 20 minutes. Cool. Spread with the pie filling. Mix Cool Whip and almond and spread on top. Refrigerate.

If you have a friend worth loving,
let him know.

BREAD PUDDING I

1 loaf French bread
5 cups hot milk
4 eggs
2 cups sugar
2½ Tbsp. vanilla extract
4 Tbsp. margarine, melted
1 cup raisins

Whiskey Sauce
1 stick of margarine or
   butter
1 cup superfine sugar
1 egg
2 jiggers bourbon (or to
   taste) ★

Soak bread in milk; crush with hands until well mixed. Beat eggs with wire whisk, adding sugar while whipping. Add egg mixture, vanilla and raisins to bread and stir well. Pour margarine in bottom of baking pan, add bread mixture and bake at 350° for 45-50 minutes or until firm. Serve with Whiskey sauce.
Serves 12.

Whiskey Sauce:
Cook sugar and butter in double boiler until very hot and well dissolved. Add egg, well beaten, whipping very fast so that egg doesn't curdle. Let cool and add bourbon.
★ Rum is also good.

This is one of Sam and Teresa's favorites. I can usually get my way if I fix them Bread Pudding.

BREAD PUDDING II

7 slices bread
6 Tbsp. sugar
3½ cups milk
4 eggs, separated
1 Tbsp. vanilla
Pinch salt
White raisins
Rum sauce (recipe follows)

Rum Sauce
½ cup sugar
¼ cup water
1 tsp. vanilla
4 Tbsp. butter
1 Tbsp. flour
2 jiggers white rum or to
   taste

Break bread into oven-proof dish, soften with a small amount of the milk. Beat sugar and egg yolks; add milk and stir well. Add vanilla and salt. Pour milk mixture over bread. Fold in raisins. Bake at 300° for 1 hour. Make a meringue with the 4 egg whites and spread on top. Bake until golden brown.

Rum Sauce:
Cook until thick, serve over warm pudding.

This comes from our very dear friend, Boty. Boty is a very vivacious lady, wonderful cook and is always smiling. Thanks, we love you, Boty. (Sam's best friend).

CHERRY COBBLER

2 (16 oz) cans pitted red
  cherries
3 Tbsp. cornstarch
¾ cup sugar
3 Tbsp. butter
1 Tbsp. grated lemon rind
¾ tsp. almond extract
½ cup sliced almonds
1 cup flour
¾ cup sugar
1 tsp. baking powder
¼ tsp. salt
½ cup milk
¼ cup shortening
1 tsp. almond extract
1 egg

Drain cherries, reserving 1 cup juice. Combine cornstarch, ¾ cup sugar and juice in a saucepan; cook on medium, stirring constantly until thick and smooth. Remove from heat and add butter, rind, and ¾ tsp. almond, stirring until butter melts. Carefully stir in cherries. Pour into a greased 12x8 baking dish. Sprinkle with sliced almonds. Combine flour, ¾ cup sugar, baking powder and salt. Add milk, shortening and almond, beat 2 minutes with a mixer. Add egg, beat 2 more minutes. Spoon evenly over cherry mixture. Bake at 350° for 35-45 minutes.
Serves 8.

FROZEN MARBLED MOUSSE

6 oz German sweet
  chocolate
3 oz unsweetened
  chocolate
10 egg yolks
1 cup sugar
3 Tbsp. dark rum
1 tsp. vanilla
2 cups whipping cream
¾ cup chopped, slivered
  almonds
1 cup whipping cream,
  beaten stiff
Grated milk chocolate

Break up both chocolates and melt in a double boiler over medium heat. Stir until smooth. Cool. Beat yolks in an electric mixer, add sugar 1 tablespoon at a time. Beat until pale yellow and a ribbon forms when beaters are lifted. Mix in rum and vanilla. Beat ½ of yolk mixture into chocolate. Whip 2 cups cream until soft peaks form. Beat ½ of cream mixture into chocolate. Fold other half into yolk mixture. Fold almonds into chocolate mixture. Drop tablespoons of each alternately into a 9-inch springform pan. Swirl with a knife. Cover and freeze overnight. Run knife around sides of pan and dip pan in hot water for 20 seconds. Invert onto a sheet of foil. Tap pan to release. Transfer to serving platter, mound whipped cream in center and garnish with grated chocolate.

FROZEN CHOCOLATE MOUSSE

1 cup sliced almonds
(6) Stella D'oro almond
  toast
3 Tbsp. melted butter
3 Tbsp. sugar
1 qt. softened vanilla ice
  cream
1 tsp. vanilla
8 oz semi-sweet chocolate
3 eggs, separated
2 Tbsp. rum
1½ cups whipping cream

Toast almonds at 350° for 15 minutes. In a food processor grind almond toast and ½ cup almonds. Combine almond mixture with melted butter and 1 Tbsp. sugar. Press evenly in a 10-inch springform pan. Bake at 350° for 10 minutes. Cool and freeze. Soften ice cream and blend in vanilla; spoon evenly over frozen crust and return to freezer. Melt chocolate in a double boiler, remove from heat. Beat egg yolks and blend into the chocolate. Add rum and set aside. Beat egg whites until soft peaks form. Gradually beat in remaining 2 Tbsp. sugar. Set aside. In a separate mixing bowl, whip 1 cup of cream into soft peaks. With a whisk blend egg whites with chocolate mixture. Fold whipped cream into mixture along with remaining almonds. Pour mousse over ice cream and freeze until firm. Whip remaining cream and decorate top with a pastry tube or spoon over when ready to serve. Cut in wedges to serve.
Serves 12.

WHITE CHOCOLATE MOUSSE

½ lb. white chocolate
3 cups whipping cream
1 envelope unflavored
  gelatin
3 egg yolks
1 egg
½ cup sugar
2 tsp. Amaretto

Melt chocolate and 1 cup cream in top of a double boiler over medium heat. Stir until smooth and melted, cool 20 minutes. Dissolve gelatin in 1 ounce warm water; add to chocolate. Beat egg yolks, egg, sugar and Amaretto until mixture turns white. In another bowl whip 2 cups cream until thickened. Combine the chocolate and egg mixtures; fold all into whipped cream. Cover and refrigerate at least 3 hours. Serve with raspberry or strawberry sauce. (Recipe for sauces in the cookbook, also).
Serves 10.

LEMON LAYER DESSERT

1st Layer:
1½ cups flour
1 stick melted margarine
¾ cup chopped pecans

2nd Layer:
8 oz softened cream
    cheese
1 cup powdered sugar
8 oz Cool Whip

3rd Layer:
1 cup sugar
¼ cup plus 1 Tbsp.
    cornstarch
⅛ tsp. salt
1½ cups boiling water
3 egg yolks
¼ cup lemon juice
2 Tbsp. grated lemon rind

4th Layer:
½ pint whipping cream
2 tsp. powdered sugar
½ tsp. lemon extract

1st Layer:
Mix together and pat into a 9x13 pan. Bake at 350° for 15 minutes. Cool.

2nd Layer:
Mix together and spread over cooled crust.

3rd Layer:
Combine sugar, cornstarch and salt in a saucepan, mix well. Stir in boiling water; cook over low heat, stirring constantly, until thickened. Combine egg yolks, lemon juice and rind; beat well. Gradually stir about ¼ of hot mixture, into yolks, add to remaining hot mixture, stirring constantly. Cook, stirring constantly, 10 minutes until smooth and thickened. Cool and put on top of cream cheese layer.

4th Layer:
Beat together until whipped and fluffy. Layer on top of custard filling. Refrigerate at least 6 hours.

BUTTERSCOTCH SQUARES

1 cup sifted flour
¼ cup quick-cook oats
¼ cup brown sugar
½ cup butter
1 cup chopped nuts
1 (12 oz) jar butterscotch
    ice cream topping
1 qt. Dutch chocolate ice
    cream

Combine flour, oats and brown sugar. Cut in butter until mixture resembles coarse crumbs. Stir in nuts. Place in a 13x9 baking pan and bake at 400° for 15 minutes. Stir while warm to crumble. Cool. Spread ½ crumb mixture in a 9x9x2 pan, drizzle ½ of topping over crumbs. Stir ice cream to soften. Spoon carefully into pan. Drizzle with remaining topping and sprinkle with remaining crumbs. Freeze. Remove about 5-10 minutes before serving.

NAPOLEONS

3 sheets Pepperidge Farms
   puff pastry, thawed

Custard:
1 qt. milk
2 tsp. vanilla
1 cup flour
1 cup sugar
6 egg yolks
½ cup cold milk
½ pint whipping cream

Icing:
3 egg whites
½ cup sugar
2 Tbsp. white corn syrup
1/16 tsp. cream of tartar
½ tsp. vanilla
¼ cup melted semi-sweet
   chocolate

Custard:
Mix together flour, sugar, egg yolks and ½ cup cold milk. Bring 1 quart milk and vanilla to a boil. Add other mixture to this and cook over medium heat for 3-4 minutes. Cool. Whip cream and fold into cooled mixture.

Icing:
Mix all ingredients (except vanilla and chocolate) together and place over boiling water for about 6 minutes, stirring with finger until too hot to do so. Remove from heat. Beat vigorously with mixer until icing holds shape, about 10 minutes. Blend in vanilla.
Roll out puff pastry to about ⅛ inch thick and 12 inches long. Prick with fork. Bake on a baking sheet at 350° for about 15-20 minutes. To assemble, layer 1 sheet of baked pastry on a platter, add custard, repeat. Top with third layer and ice. Drizzle top with chocolate. Serves 12-16. Cut with a serrated knife.

This takes a little time but is well worth it. It will impress anyone!

STRAWBERRY CHIFFON SQUARES

¼ cup margarine
1½ cups vanilla wafer
   crumbs
3 oz package strawberry
   jello
¾ cup boiling water
1 can condensed milk
10 oz package frozen
   strawberries, thawed
4 cups miniature
   marshmallows
Small container Cool whip
1 pint fresh strawberries,
   sliced

Melt the butter and mix with the vanilla wafer crumbs; pat in the bottom of an 11x7 dish. Chill. Dissolve jello in boiling water; stir in condensed milk and frozen strawberries. Fold in marshmallows and Cool Whip. Pour on top of crust. Chill at least 2 hours. Garnish with fresh strawberries and additional Cool Whip if desired.

STRAWBERRY TRIFLE

1 can Eagle Brand
   condensed milk
1½ cups cold water
1 small pkg. French vanilla
   instant pudding
1 pint whipping cream,
   whipped with 1 tsp.
   almond extract
1 (13½ oz) pound cake, cut
   into cubes
1 qt. fresh strawberries,
   washed & sliced
¾ cup strawberry
   preserves
Additional fresh
   strawberries for garnish
½ cup toasted, slivered
   almonds

In large bowl, combine condensed milk and water. Add pudding mix and beat well. Chill 5 minutes. Fold in whipped cream. Spoon 2 cups of mixture in bottom of a glass bowl; top with half the cake cubes, half the strawberries, half the preserves and more pudding. Repeat and top with pudding. Garnish with additional strawberries and almonds. Chill thoroughly.

PAM'S SPUMONI

1½ pints French vanilla ice
   cream
Rum flavoring
6 cherries
1½ pints pistachio ice
   cream
¾ cup whipping cream
⅓ cup Nestle' Quick
10 oz package frozen
   strawberries
½ cup whipping cream
¼ cup powdered sugar

Chill a 2 quart metal bowl in freezer. Stir the French vanilla ice cream to soften, add rum flavoring. Refreeze until workable. With chilled spoon spread quickly in layer over bottom and sides of chilled bowl, all the way to top. Refreeze if it tends to slip. Circle cherries around bottom, freeze until firm. Stir pistachio until softened; refreeze until workable. Spread over sides and top of first layer. Freeze till firm. Combine ¾ cup cream and chocolate; whip to peaks. Spread over pistachio; freeze. Drain strawberries. Mix ½ cup cream, powdered sugar and a dash of salt; whip to peaks. Fold strawberries into whipped cream; pile in center of mold; smooth top. (May need to add more ice cream). Cover with foil and freeze 6 hours.
Peel off foil; invert onto chilled plate. Rub bowl with towel rung out in hot water to loosen, lift bowl.
Serves 12-16.

Dee Reiser
(713) 358-4208

Best of Friends

P.O. Box 5573
Kingwood, Texas 77325

Feb. 2, 1989

Menu

Chicken Piccata
BOF Two P. 109

Wild Rice Dressing
BOF P. 60

Peas With Sweet Basil
BOF Two P. 78

Spiced Peach Salad
BOF Two P. 57

Finger Rolls
BOF P. 19

Red Velvet Cake (Recipe on back)
BOF P. 99

Teresa Dormer
(713) 359-6733

Red Velvet Cake

1½ c. sugar
½ c. shortening
2 eggs
2 c. flour
1 tsp. salt
2 Tbsp. cocoa
1 c. buttermilk
2 oz red food coloring
1½ tsp. vanilla
1 tsp. soda in 1 Tbsp. vinegar

Cream shortening & sugar; add eggs & beat well. Sift flour, salt & cocoa 3 times; add alternately to creamed mixture with buttermilk. Add vanilla & coloring. Fold in soda & vinegar (do not beat). Bake in 3 (9") greased & floured pans at 350° for 25-30 minutes. Cool.

Icing

1 c. milk
1 c. sugar
¼ tsp. salt
¼ c. flour
1 c. butter
2 tsp. vanilla
1 c. flaked coconut

Mix flour & salt with milk until blended; cook slowly until very thick. Cool thoroughly! Cream butter & sugar until fluffy; then add to cooled mixture & beat well (looks like whipped cream). Add vanilla. Put on cake & garnish with coconut (be sure your cake is cold so icing won't melt).

ELEGANT STRAWBERRY CREPES

Crepes:
4 eggs
1 cup sifted flour
1 cup milk
Grated rind of 1 orange
2 Tbsp. brandy
2 Tbsp. melted butter
1 Tbsp. sugar
½ tsp. salt
Additional butter

Filling:
16 oz softened cream
   cheese
Grated rind of 1 orange
3 Tbsp. sugar
3 Tbsp. whipping cream

Sauce:
½ cup butter
½ cup sugar
Juice of 1 orange
Juice of ½ lemon
¼ cup brandy
¼ cup orange liqueur
¼ cup peach brandy
1 pint strawberries, mashed
1 pint strawberries, halved

Crepes:
Combine all ingredients in blender and whirl until completely mixed. Refrigerate at least 1 hour. Heat a crepe pan and brush bottom with butter. For each crepe, pour 2-3 Tbsp. battter in pan, swirling around until it covers entire bottom. Cook over medium heat 1-2 minutes, turn and cook 30 seconds. Stack on a towel.

Filling:
Combine all ingredients in a processor and mix well.

Sauce:
Heat a large skillet and add butter. When melted, blend in sugar, orange and lemon juices and all liqueurs. Add mashed strawberries and stir until sauce is bubbling.

To assemble: place 1 tablespoon of filling along one side of each crepe. Roll crepes and arrange on a platter. Refrigerate at least 1 hour. To serve, put some sliced strawberries on a dessert plate, then crepes, spoon the warm sauce over. Allow 2 crepes per serving. Any leftover crepes may be frozen.

FUDGE SAUCE

½ cup butter
2¼ cups powdered sugar
⅔ cup evaporated milk
6 squares unsweetened
   chocolate
½ tsp. vanilla

In a double boiler mix together butter and powdered sugar; add evaporated milk and chocolate. Cook over hot water for 30 minutes. DO NOT STIR. Remove from heat, add vanilla and beat. Add a little cream if it seems too thick. Store in the refrigerator and heat as needed. Makes excellent gifts.

CHERRY PUDDING

10 Tbsp. cake flour
10 Tbsp. powdered sugar
½ tsp. salt
3 large eggs, lightly beaten
3 cups half & half, scalded
  and cooled
1 can dark, sweet, pitted
  cherries
1 tsp. almond extract,
  divided
Powdered sugar
1 can cherry pie filling

Sift flour, sugar and salt into a mixing bowl. Make a well in the center and pour in eggs. Stir half & half into the eggs. Using a wooden spoon, mix a very small amount of the flour at a time with liquid. Mixture must be very smooth. Gradually add dark cherries and ½ tsp. almond extract to the mixture, mixing with a wooden spoon. Pour into a well-greased casserole and bake at 400° for 40 minutes or until top is delicately browned. Sprinkle with powdered sugar. Can be served warm or cold. Warm cherry pie filling with ½ tsp. almond extract added and pour over top of pudding.

Very good!

BUTTER CRISPS

2 cups sifted flour
¼ lb. butter
1 egg yolk
¾ cup sour cream
2 Tbsp. melted butter
¾ cup sugar
1 tsp. cinnamon
¾ cup chopped nuts

Cut butter into flour with a fork. Add egg yolk and sour cream. Mix well. When blended shape into a ball. Sprinkle with flour and wrap in plastic wrap. Chill several hours. Combine sugar, cinnamon and nuts. Spread board lightly with flour. Divide dough into 4 parts. Roll out one at a time into a large circle about ¼ inch thick. Brush with melted butter and sprinkle with the sugar mixture. cut into 10-12 wedges; roll up starting at widest end. Bake on a greased baking sheet at 375° for 20 minutes.

Dee likes these just fine as is, but for those of us with a real sweet tooth they are even better with a powdered sugar glaze.

If you have one true friend you have more
than your share.

BEV'S MUNCHIES

1½ cups packed brown
  sugar
½ cup butter, softened
1½ tsp. vanilla
2 eggs
1¾ cups flour
2 tsp. baking powder
Dash salt
2 squares unsweetened
  chocolate, melted &
  cooled
1 package Butter Brickle
1 cup sugar
5 Tbsp. butter
⅓ cup milk
1 cup semi-sweet chocolate
  chips

In a large bowl, cream brown sugar and ½ cup butter. Blend in vanilla and eggs; mix well. Stir in flour, baking powder and salt; mix well. Divide dough into 2 parts; stir chocolate into half of dough. Grease a 9x13 inch pan. Drop each dough randomly into pan by table-spoons. Marble with a knife and spread evenly. Bake at 350° for 17-20 minutes or until golden brown. Cool, then freeze for about 20 minutes. In a small saucepan, combine sugar, 5 Tbsp. butter, and milk. Boil 1 minute, stirring constantly. Remove from heat; stir in chocolate chips until melted and smooth. Sprinkle the Butter Brickle over the bars. Pour the hot topping over all. Refrigerate 30 minutes; cut into bars. Store in the refrigerator.
Makes 24 bars.

Bev's specialty is desserts and anything chocolate is at the top of her list. She's one of our strongest supporters and even helps us market our first cookbook.

This is one of Jonathan's favorites!

CHEWY PECAN SQUARES

½ cup melted butter
2 cups packed brown
  sugar
2 large eggs
1 cup flour
2 tsp. baking powder
¼ tsp. salt
2 tsps. vanilla extract
1¼ cups chopped pecans
Powdered sugar

Beat together the butter and brown sugar until well blended. Add eggs, beating well. Combine flour, baking powder and salt; stir into creamed mixture. Stir in vanilla and pecans. Spoon into a greased and floured 9x13 inch pan. Bake at 350° for 25 minutes. Immediately sift powdered sugar over the top. Cool and cut into squares.
Makes 2 dozen.

SWEET DREAMS

1 cup unsalted butter
1½ cups packed brown sugar
1 egg, room temperature
1 tsp. vanilla
2 cups flour
1 tsp. baking soda
1 tsp. cinnamon
1 tsp. ground ginger
½ tsp. salt
12 oz semi-sweet chocolate chips
1¼ cups chopped walnuts
1 cup powdered sugar

Cream butter, beat in sugar, egg and vanilla. Combine flour, baking soda, cinnamon, ginger and salt. Blend into butter mixture. Fold in chocolate chips and walnuts. Refrigerate until firm. Break off small pieces of dough and roll into 1-inch balls; dredge into powdered sugar. Bake on greased baking sheets at 375° for 10 minutes. Cool on sheets 5 minutes, then remove.

These are so good, Dee couldn't leave them alone.

TIGER COOKIES

6 oz chocolate chips
3 cups Kellogg's sugar frosted flakes
2 cups flour
1 tsp. baking soda
½ tsp. salt
1 cup softened butter
1 cup sugar
2 eggs
1 tsp. vanilla
1 cup chopped pecans (optional)

Melt chocolate over low heat, stirring constantly. Crush frosted flakes and set aside. Sift together flour, soda and salt. Cream butter and sugar until light and fluffy. Add eggs and vanilla and beat well. Add sifted dry ingredients; mix well. Fold in frosted flakes and pecans. Swirl warm melted chocolate through batter. Drop by tablespoonfuls onto ungreased baking sheets. Bake at 375° for 12 minutes.
Makes 5 dozen cookies.

PECAN ICEBOX COOKIES

2 sticks margarine
1 cup granulated sugar
1 cup brown sugar
2 eggs, well beaten
1 tsp. salt
1 tsp. soda
1-1½ tsp. vanilla
2 cups chopped pecans
4 cups flour

Cream margarine and sugars well. Add eggs, soda, salt and vanilla. Add pecans and mix well. Gradually stir in flour until thoroughly mixed. Divide dough into 6 parts. Roll in wax paper and refrigerate until cold and firm. Cut cookies about ⅛" thick. Bake at 350° for 8-10 minutes.
Makes about 16 dozen cookies.

ALMOND CHEESECAKE COOKIES

cup

½ lb. butter, softened
3 oz package cream
  cheese
l cup sugar
1 cup flour
½ cup, broken, sliced
  almonds

Cream together butter and cream cheese, gradually add sugar, beating until light and fluffy. Add flour and beat well. Stir in almonds. Roll dough into 1" balls, place on an ungreased cookie sheet about 2" apart. Dip the bottom of a glass in water and gently press each cookie until 2" in diameter. Bake at 375° for 10-12 minutes. Cool before removing.
Makes 2½ dozen.

PUMPKIN BARS

2 cups sugar
l cup oil
4 eggs
2 cups cooked pumpkin
2 cups flour
2 tsp. baking powder
1 tsp. baking soda
¼ tsp. salt
2 tsp. cinnamon
l tsp. pumpkin-pie spice
Chopped pecans, optional

Frosting:
3 oz cream cheese
¼ cup butter
l tsp. vanilla
2 cups powdered sugar
1-2 tsp. milk

In a mixer beat sugar and oil. Add eggs, one at a time, beat well. Add pumpkin, flour, baking powder, baking soda, salt, cinnamon and pie spice. Beat well. Spread in a 15x10 inch pan. Bake at 350° for 25 minutes. Cool and frost. (recipe follows)

Frosting:
Beat all ingredients well and spread on cool bars. Sprinkle with chopped pecans if desired.

SKILLET COOKIES

¾ cup sugar
¾ cup white corn syrup
3 Tbsp. butter
¾ cup peanut butter
4 cups Rice Krispies

In a large skillet boil together sugar, syrup and butter for l minute. Remove from heat and stir in peanut butter, mixing well. Stir in Rice Krispies. Drop by spoonfuls onto wax paper.

Kids love these!

NANA'S VANITY'S

3 egg yolks
3 Tbsp. cream
1 tsp. sugar
Pinch salt
1 cup flour
Powdered sugar
(May use 2 Tbsp. cream &
   1 Tbsp. brandy instead of
   3 Tbsp. cream)

Mix yolks, cream, sugar, salt and flour to make a dough stiff enough to roll. Roll out on board and cut in 3 inch squares. Make a slit in center and pull 1 corner through. Fry in hot grease, turning once. Sprinkle with powdered sugar.

MARTHA'S CINNAMON BARS

1 cup butter
1 cup sugar
1 egg, separated
2 cups flour
4 tsp. ground cinnamon
1 cup minced pecans

Cream butter and sugar thoroughly in large bowl of mixer. Add egg yolk, then flour sifted with cinnamon. Pat into an ungreased 15x10 inch pan; pour unbeaten egg white over surface; drain off excess. Sprinkle nuts over top, pressing them down lightly with palm of hand. Bake at 325° for 25-30 minutes. Cut into bars while hot.

GLAZED SPICE BARS

¾ cup oil
¼ cup honey
1 cup sugar
1 egg
2 cups flour
½ tsp. salt
1 tsp. soda
1½ tsp. cinnamon
1 cup chopped pecans
Glaze (recipe follows)

Combine all ingredients except glaze, and mix well. (Makes a stiff dough). Pat into an ungreased 13x9 inch pan. Bake at 350° for 25-30 minutes. Spread glaze over top while hot. Makes about 48 squares.

Glaze:
Combine all ingredients, whisking until smooth.

Glaze:
1 cup powdered sugar
1½ tsp. vanilla
1 Tbsp. mayonnaise
1 Tbsp. water

A friend knows it's okay to need as well as to be needed.

ROCKY ROAD BARS

Base:
½ cup margarine
1 square unsweetened
  chocolate
1 cup flour
1 cup sugar
1 tsp. baking powder
1 tsp. vanilla
2 eggs
¾ cup chopped nuts

Filling:
6 oz softened cream
  cheese
¼ cup softened margarine
½ cup sugar
2 Tbsp. flour
½ tsp. vanilla
1 egg
½ cup chopped nuts
6 oz semi-sweet chocolate
  chips

Frosting:
2 cups miniature
  marshmallows
¼ cup margarine
¼ cup milk
1 square unsweetened
  chocolate
2 oz softened cream
  cheese
3 cups sifted powdered
  sugar
1 tsp. vanilla

Base:
In a large saucepan over low heat, melt margarine and chocolate, stirring constantly until well blended. Add flour and remaining base ingredients; mix well. Spread into a greased and floured 9x13 pan.

Filling:
In a small bowl, combine all filling ingredients except nuts and chips. Beat 1 minute at medium speed until smooth and fluffy; stir in nuts. Spread over chocolate mixture and sprinkle evenly with chocolate chips.
Bake at 350° for 25-35 minutes.

Frosting:
As soon as cake comes out of oven sprinkle marshmallows over top. Return to oven and bake an additional 2 minutes. In large saucepan over low heat combine margarine, milk, chocolate and cream cheese, stirring until well blended. Remove from heat; stir in powdered sugar and vanilla until smooth. Immediately pour frosting over marshmallows and lightly swirl to marble with knife. Refrigerate until firm; cut into bars.

Mary brought this jewel back to us from a trip to Baton Rouge.

There is no better looking-glass than
an old friend.

CHERRY CHEESE BARS

Crust:
1 cup pecans, divided
1¼ cups flour
½ cup brown sugar, firmly
packed
½ cup margarine, soft
½ cup coconut

Filling:
1 (8 oz) pkg. cream
cheese, softened
⅓ cup sugar
1 egg
1 tsp. almond extract
1 can cherry pie filling

Chop ½ cup pecans finely for crust and ½ cup coarsely for the topping. Combine flour and brown sugar. Cut in margarine until fine crumb texture. Add finely chopped nuts and coconut. Mix well; remove ½ cup and set aside. Press remaining crumbs in bottom of greased 9x13 pan. Bake in preheated 350° oven for 12-15 minutes or until edges are lightly browned. Beat cream cheese, sugar, egg and almond extract until smooth. Spread over hot crust and return to oven. Bake 10 minutes. Spread cherry pie filling over cheese layer. Combine reserved coarsely chopped nuts and reserved crumbs. Sprinkle evenly over cherries. Return to oven and bake 15 minutes longer. Let cool.
Makes 24 bars.

Another good recipe from Mary.

FUDGE BROWNIES

1¼ cups sugar
1 stick butter
4 eggs
1 can Hershey's syrup
1 cup flour
¾ cup chopped nuts
Icing (recipe follows)

Icing
6 Tbsp. butter
6 Tbsp. milk
1¼ cups powdered sugar
½ cup chocolate chips
½ cup chopped nuts

Cream together the sugar and butter. Add eggs, one at a time, beating well after each. Add syrup and flour alternately to mixture. Stir in nuts. Pour into a greased 11x15 pan. Bake at 350° for 15-20 minutes. Remove from oven, cool 15 minutes and ice.

Icing:
Mix butter, milk and sugar in a saucepan. Over medium heat bring to a boil. Boil 1 minute. Add chocolate chips and nuts. Beat with a wooden spoon. Refrigerate a few minutes and beat more. Spread on brownies.

JULIE'S CHOCOLATE PEANUT CRUNCH

4 cups Quick oats
¼ cup sugar
1 cup brown sugar
1 cup margarine, melted
1 (6 oz) pkg. chocolate
chips
1 cup peanut butter

In large bowl, combine oats, sugars, and margarine. Mix and put in 13x9 pan. Bake at 350° for 15 minutes. *Do not overcook.* Mixture firms as it cools. Make sure it is cool before you put topping on. Melt chocolate and mix in peanut butter. Spread on top of oat mixture. These are like Granola Bars.

Kathy from Cypresswood gave this recipe to us. It's a great tennis snack. Everyone likes it. Thanks, Kathy, for sharing with us. We also enjoyed the tennis match.

CARAMEL CORN

15 cups popped corn
1 cup light brown sugar
¼ cup corn syrup
½ cup margarine
½ tsp. salt
½ tsp. soda
1 Tbsp. vanilla

Heat sugar, syrup, margarine and salt until it bubbles, stirring. Cook 5 minutes. Remove from heat, add soda and vanilla. Pour over popcorn and coat evenly. Spread on greased cookie sheet. Bake at 200° for 1 hour. Stir every 15 minutes.
May add nuts to mixture if desired.

CHERRY CORDIALS

½ cup maraschino
cherries with stems
½ cup brandy
5 oz semi-sweet chocolate

Drain cherries and soak in brandy overnight. Drain and place cherries in freezer. When frozen, melt chocolate over hot water. Dry cherries and dip in chocolate. Place on wax paper. Chill.

ENGLISH TOFFEE

½ lb. butter
1 cup sugar
3 tsp. water
1 cup chopped nuts
3 Hershey bars

Combine butter, sugar and water in a heavy saucepan and boil, stirring constantly until the color of light brown sugar. The length of cooking time is not critical. Add the nuts. Pour onto a greased platter. Place the candy bars on the hot toffee and spread the melting chocolate over the toffee. Cool before breaking into pieces. (Will harden better in the refrigerator).

SPICED PECANS

1 egg white
2 Tbsp. water
½ cup sugar
¼ tsp. cinnamon
¼ tsp. cloves
¼ tsp. allspice
2 cups pecan halves

Mix all ingredients except pecans, stirring well. Stir in pecans, coating evenly. Spread on a greased baking sheet. Bake at 250° for about 20 minutes or until dry.

PEANUT BUTTER CANDY

1 stick margarine, softened
1 cup peanut butter
¾ box powdered sugar
6 oz package chocolate
  chips
1 Tbsp. margarine

Mix together 1 stick margarine and peanut butter; pat into a microwave-proof square dish. Cook on high 1½ minutes. Add powdered sugar and mix well. Melt together the chocolate chips and 1 Tbsp. margarine on medium. Spread on top of the peanut butter filling. Refrigerate for only 15 minutes.

CANDIED APPLES

6 apples
2 cups sugar
1 cup water
¾ cup light Karo syrup
½ tsp. cinnamon
Red food coloring

Stir sugar, syrup and water until dissolved. Cover and bring to a boil on low heat. Uncover. Bring to a rapid boil and boil until mixture is brittle when dropped in water. Do not stir while cooking. After it's brittle, add cinnamon and food coloring. Dip apples in mixture and set on wax paper.
Makes 6.

BUTTERFINGERS

1½ boxes Wheat Thin
  Crackers (original)
Creamy peanut butter
1 lb. Guittard's milk
  chocolate chips, melted

Spread a small amount of peanut butter between two Wheat Thin crackers making a sandwich. Dip the sandwich in chocolate and place on wax paper to harden. Makes a bunch.

Thanks, Mary these are great!

INDEX

Notes

Notes

Best of Friends Two
P.O. Box 5573
Kingwood, Texas 77325

Please send me _____ copies of **Best of Friends Two** at $9.95 plus $1.50 for postage and handling per copy. Texas residents add $.61 sales tax.

Please send me _____ copies of **Best of Friends** at $9.95 plus $1.50 for postage and handling per copy. Texas residents add $.61 sales tax.

Make check payable to Best of Friends.
Enclosed is my check or money order for $ _____ .

Name _____

Address _____

City _____ State _____ Zip Code _____

Best of Friends Two
P.O. Box 5573
Kingwood, Texas 77325

Please send me _____ copies of **Best of Friends Two** at $9.95 plus $1.50 for postage and handling per copy. Texas residents add $.61 sales tax.

Please send me _____ copies of **Best of Friends** at $9.95 plus $1.50 for postage and handling per copy. Texas residents add $.61 sales tax.

Make check payable to Best of Friends.
Enclosed is my check or money order for $ _____ .

Name _____

Address _____

City _____ State _____ Zip Code _____

Best of Friends Two
P.O. Box 5573
Kingwood, Texas 77325

Please send me _____ copies of **Best of Friends Two** at $9.95 plus $1.50 for postage and handling per copy. Texas residents add $.61 sales tax.

Please send me _____ copies of **Best of Friends** at $9.95 plus $1.50 for postage and handling per copy. Texas residents add $.61 sales tax.

Make check payable to Best of Friends.
Enclosed is my check or money order for $ _____ .

Name _____

Address _____

City _____ State _____ Zip Code _____

Reorder Additional Copies